THE FUTURE OF HUMAN RIGHTS IN THE UNITED KINGDOM:
ESSAYS ON LAW AND PRACTICE

31/10/97

This book is to be returned on o.
the last date stamped below.

The Future of Human Rights in the United Kingdom: Essays on Law and Practice

RABINDER SINGH

B.A. (CANTAB), LL.M. (CALIFORNIA)

Barrister

·HART·
PUBLISHING

OXFORD

1997

Hart Publishing
Oxford
UK

© Rabinder Singh 1997

Distributed in North America by
Northwestern University Press
625 Colfax, Evanston IL
60208-4210 USA

Hart Publishing is a specialist legal publisher based in Oxford, England.
To order further copies of this book or to request a list of other
publications please write to:

Hart Publishing, 19 Whitehouse Road, Oxford, OX1 4PA
Telephone: +44 (0)1865 434459 or Fax: (0)1865 794882
e-mail: hartpub@janep.demon.co.uk

British Library Cataloguing in Publication Data
Data Available
ISBN 1–901362–20–5

Typeset in 10pt Sabon
by SetAll, Abingdon
Printed in Great Britain on acid-free paper
by Biddles Ltd. Guildford and King's Lynn

*This book is dedicated to my mother
and to the memory of my father*

Foreword

This is a book with a theme both topical and perennial; topical because the Labour Government has pledged to introduce the European Convention on Human Rights ("ECHR") into domestic law; perennial because the rights enjoyed by human beings as human beings are as important an index of the moral health and emotional welfare of any society as can be found.

Precisely how the ECHR will be incorporated is at the time of writing unknown. But the second essay in this collection will provide a check list for legislators and a measuring rod for critics: Mr Singh favours a semi-hard model, giving the incorporation Act superior but not unrepealable status.

Much of the motive force for incorporation has come from the senior judges themselves; and in his essay on the protection of privacy in English law, Mr Singh depicts a new frontier which they are already patrolling. Although an eloquent proponent of the view that democracy and human rights are not only compatible but complementary, Mr Singh argues the case for regarding unelected judges as the vital custodians of both; and in his first essay demonstrates the way in which the modern judiciary have in the field of public law "woken the common law from its long slumber and started to reclaim their human rights heritage".

But judges can only dispose; it is for litigants to propose and in his concluding essay, "The Future of Public Interest Litigation", Mr Singh identifies gaps and makes proposals for ensuring not merely that the rules on locus standi should remain liberalised but that rules should be modified to permit third party intervention in appropriate cases and that the traditional sanction of costs against the losing party should be abandoned where it was in the public interest for the point to be tested.

With two further essays on fundamental rights of expression and free movement, Mr Singh has constructed seven pillars of wisdom. Mr Singh's familiarity with politics, literature and philosophy adds context to his analysis and strength to his arguments, as does his use of comparative law. It is interesting to note that some of the material for the book relates to cases in which he has been involved as an advocate: there could be no better illustration of the value of interplay between the theoretical and the practical.

June 1997

The Honourable Michael J. Beloff Q.C.
Trinity College, Oxford
and 4–5 Gray's Inn Square

Contents

Preface and Acknowledgements

The idea for this book came from a series of seminars which I had the pleasure of giving as a Visiting Fellow at Queen Mary and Westfield College, London in late 1996 and early 1997. I would like to thank Lord Steyn, His Honour Judge David Pearl and Lord Lester of Herne Hill QC, who chaired those public symposia (on cold and wet evenings); and Professor Genevra Richardson, Professor John Yelland and Geraldine Van Bueren, who organised them. I would also like to thank everyone who attended those seminars, including students, practitioners and judges. Although it is invidious to name particular people, I am especially grateful to Sir Stephen Sedley, Sir Alan Moses, Nicholas Blake QC and Stephen Grosz for taking part in one or more of the seminars. Finally I would like to thank Professor Peter Hennessy for taking the time to come away from his own busy schedule elsewhere at QMW to attend the first seminar. As I suggest in this book, the idea of human rights is essentially political and philosophical in origin: law is merely one of the techniques by which that noble idea may be realised. The involvement of scholars from other disciplines is vital if we are to have a human rights culture in the United Kingdom.

A number of people asked if the papers I gave at QMW would be published: they now appear as Chapters 3, 6 and 7 of this book. It occurred to me that, to put some of the ideas in those papers in context, readers might find it helpful to have in one place a number of other papers I have written on the topic of public law and human rights. I hope that it will be apparent from the text that certain themes run through each of the chapters, as I try to outline in the Introduction. I have revised and updated the essays where appropriate, while trying to keep the sense and style of the original.

The only essay that has been previously published is Chapter 4, which appeared in an earlier version in [1988] PL 212. I would like to thank again Professor D. J. Harris of the University of Nottingham for his comments on a draft of that article. I would also like to thank Sweet & Maxwell for their permission to reproduce a revised version of that article here.

Thanks are due to everyone at my chambers, in particular to Murray Hunt for his comments on draft chapters of this book; Karen Steyn, who invited me to give a talk to Young Justice (see Chapter 1 of this book); Marie Demetriou for her comments on Chapter 6; Andrew Tabachnik for his help with the writing of Chapters 6 and 7; Andrew Sharland, who helped to update and check the references, in particular in Chapter 4; and Ann Kavanagh, who helped with the typing. Thanks are also due to Pavlos Eleftheriadis of QMW for his comments on Chapter 3; and to Philip Leach (solicitor at Liberty) for his help with Chapter 5.

I owe immeasurable gratitude to Michael Beloff QC (joint head of our chambers and President of Trinity College, Oxford), who has been an inspiration since the day I met him as a student in 1984 and who was kind enough to write the Foreword to this book; and to Sir Alan Moses (now a High Court judge) who gave me many of the breaks that a young barrister needs and who, in the best traditions of the Bar, acted for all who instructed him with courage, no matter how unpopular their cause (including the then government).

It was my great good fortune that, just when the idea for publication of these papers was suggested to me, Hart Publishing was beginning its exciting venture of producing books that, I hope, will bridge the gap between the academic and the practising branches of the legal community. I am very grateful to Richard Hart and Jane Parker for their encouragement and professionalism and wish them well in that project.

Last but not least I owe many thanks to my wife, Alison Baigent, and to our two sons: all of them tolerate not only my career at the Bar but the occasions at home when I leave them to sit in front of a computer.

Finally I should say a word about the title of this book. I hope that readers will not find it presumptuous of me to talk of the future of human rights in the United Kingdom when (as will be apparent from the titles of some of the chapters) my experience extends only to English law. I hope that many of the suggestions that I make for the future will have relevance to the other legal systems in the United Kingdom: in the case of the incorporation of the European Convention on Human Rights (Chapter 2) this will be so directly but I hope that it may also be true indirectly of what I say elsewhere in the book.

RABINDER SINGH

4–5 Gray's Inn Square
May Day 1997

Table of United Kingdom Cases

TABLE OF CASES FROM OTHER JURISDICTIONS

Canada

European Commission and Court of Human Rights

European Court of Justice

New Zealand

United States

TABLE OF UNITED KINGDOM LEGISLATION

TABLE OF LEGISLATION FROM OTHER JURISDICTIONS

TABLE OF INTERNATIONAL INSTRUMENTS

Introduction

"All human beings are born free and equal in dignity and rights."
Article 1 of the Universal Declaration of Human Rights

If the twentieth century has a "big idea" it is the idea of human rights. As I suggest in Chapter 3 of this book, the achievement of the twentieth century has been the establishment of an international code of universal human rights. The task for the coming century will be to make those rights effective – and effective not just for a few, but for everyone on an equal basis, true to the spirit of the above quotation from the Universal Declaration of Human Rights.

Lawyers in the United Kingdom have not traditionally been at ease with the language of fundamental rights. This is disappointing since, as I outline in Chapter 1 of this book, this country has played an enviable role over the centuries in devising and exporting the idea of human rights. This is, after all, the land where Tom Paine was born. It is not, however, surprising that lawyers have found that the language of rights does not come readily to them. This is also the land from which Paine was banished. Legal education and practice in this country have for two centuries been influenced by three men whose legacy will, I believe, ultimately be judged to have been a detrimental one: Bentham, the founder of Utilitarianism, who famously declared that talk of rights was nonsense and talk of natural rights "nonsense upon stilts";[1] Austin, who propounded the positivist view of law,[2] which draws a rigid distinction between law and morality but which ultimately breaks down, as every practitioner knows, since hard cases are not decided according to pure "legal doctrine", which is separate from morality, but according to the judge's sense of the justice of the case; and Dicey, who more or less invented the doctrine of parliamentary sovereignty,[3] which leaves the United Kingdom virtually alone in the democratic world with a legislature that can, it seems,

---

[1] J Bentham, *The Works of Jeremy Bentham* (J Bowring ed.) (Edinburgh, 1838–43) vol 2, at 501.

[2] J Austin, *The Province of Jurisprudence Determined* (London, Weidenfeld & Nicholson, 1954).

[3] A V Dicey, *Introduction to the Study of the Law of the Constitution* 10th edn (London, Macmillan, 1959) chs I–III.

do whatever it likes, even to the extent of violating the human rights of the people.

In the last few years, however, there has been increasing interest in human rights. This has been true not only – or even primarily – of lawyers. This is a healthy sign. Human rights are too important to be left to lawyers. The best country would be one where human rights lawyers were not needed. But sometimes, unfortunately, they will be. I hope that this book will make a small contribution to the debate in this country about the future of human rights and how best to give them effective protection for all. This is especially so as it is published in a year when a new government has been elected which is, for the first time, committed to incorporation of the European Convention on Human Rights.

Each of the essays in this book can be read in isolation: most were delivered as lectures and were intended to be comprehensible on their own. However, there are certain themes which I try to explore in this book and which I hope connect the chapters together, since they reflect my own view of human rights in this country and my hopes for the future. Those themes in outline are that:

(1) The concept of human rights is not alien to English law but was historically embedded in it. As the Lord Chief Justice has suggested, this country could once again become a teacher in the field of human rights, rather than a pupil[4] (Chapters 1, 2 and 6).

(2) English public law already, even in the absence of incorporation of the European Convention on Human Rights, has the capacity to protect human rights, albeit inadequately (Chapters 1, 3 and 5).

(3) There is no contradiction between democracy and human rights. The relationship between the different branches of the state (legislative, executive and judicial) is, however, a subtle one and the judiciary should not lose their legitimacy by straying too readily into areas where political judgment may be preferable, not because it is necessarily better but because politicians are in a democracy accountable to the people (Chapters 3 and 7).

(4) The concept of rights should not be confined to civil and political rights but should, in conformity to this country's legal obligations in international law, extend to social and economic rights (Chapter 3).

(5) The concept which lies at the heart of human rights is that of equality. The idea of equality also provides the link between democracy and human rights, since democracy rests on the essential equality of human beings, no matter what their differences in birth, wealth or education (Chapter 3).

---

[4] Lord Bingham of Cornhill CJ, "The European Convention on Human Rights: Time to Incorporate" in R Gordon & R Wilmot-Smith (eds), *Human Rights in the United Kingdom* (Oxford, Clarendon Press, 1996), ch. 1.

(6) The concept of equality in the enjoyment of rights should be given substantive content. This requires more than formal equality. For example, to give everyone the right to freedom of speech but to allow one person to control large parts of the media while others, who express themselves through peaceful demonstrations, may be guilty of criminal offences[5] violates the principle of substantive equality (Chapters 3, 4 and 7).

(7) Lawyers interested in making rights effective have available to them a variety of sources of law which, if used with imagination, can lead to unexpected opportunities: for example European Community law can be used even in the absence of incorporation of the European Convention on Human Rights to provide a fundamental law which reaches beyond commercial interests to such human rights as freedom of movement and freedom of expression (Chapter 6).

(8) Procedure matters. To make human rights effective, the procedure used by the courts should be modified to encourage and assist public interest litigation. It is possible to have the most beautiful human rights charter imaginable but it may not work. To make it work requires attention to the practical mechanics both of incorporation and of implementation (Chapters 2 and 7).

I should say a word here about the link between democracy and human rights because it is often suggested that those of us who believe in human rights are not truly committed to democracy. In fact, democracy itself, like the concept of human rights, rests on the concept of equality. Universal adult suffrage in modern societies has two aspects: first, everyone, barring some readily understandable exceptions such as peers, has the vote but, secondly, everyone has only one vote.[6] In a parliamentary election, we all count but no-one counts more than anyone else. It was not always thus. In the debates which eventually led to the Second Reform Act in 1867, it was suggested by Disraeli that some upstanding members of society should have more than one vote, for example if they were clergymen.[7] Until the special constituencies for the older universities were abolished after the Second World War, graduates of those universities could vote more than once, a privilege denied to mere mortals. Today, such notions seem archaic. Why? It is surely because we have come to accept that, however unequal society may be in fact, all of us are, in a fundamental respect, equal. We are ultimately of equal worth. We owe each

---

[5] See, for a recent example, *DPP* v. *Jones* [1997] 2 All ER 119 (DC), which concerned the offence of trespassory assembly which is committed by participants in an assembly of twenty or more persons, however peaceful it may be, within the area designated by an order made under section 14A of the Public Order Act 1986, as amended. See further Chapters 1 and 4 *infra*.

[6] Article 25(b) of the International Covenant on Civil and Political Rights (1966) refers to the right to vote at elections "which shall be by universal *and equal* suffrage" (*emphasis added*).

[7] See the excellent biography of Gladstone by Lord Jenkins of Hillhead: R Jenkins, *Gladstone* (London, Macmillan, 1995) at 269–73.

other equal concern and respect.[8] Once it is understood that democracy itself rests on this more fundamental idea, it can be seen that the concept of human rights supports democracy and is not hostile to it. This is so not only intellectually but historically, since those who advocated the sovereignty of the people in the age of revolution also wrote of the "rights of man", a phrase which in our century has belatedly been modernised to "human rights".

[8] See R Dworkin, *Taking Rights Seriously* (London, Duckworth, 1977) at 180–3 and 272–8.

1

The Protection of Human Rights in English Public Law[1]

Some years ago I had the privilege of studying in the United States on a Harkness Fellowship, a wonderfully generous programme which is sadly to end. My experience at Berkeley taught me the importance of human rights in any legal system. I learnt that there is a tradition in Anglo-American legal thought and practice, dedicated to the protection of liberty, which for many years was obscured, if not silenced, on this side of the Atlantic. So it was that, having studied law for three years in Britain, it was only when I went to America that I was first introduced to the writings of *English* thinkers on the subject of human rights. One example is John Milton, famed for his epic poetry, who also wrote many important works of prose in the seventeenth century. One of these, *The Areopagitica*, first published in 1644, provides a classic defence of freedom of the press.[2] That work is relatively little known in Milton's home country, at least to lawyers. In America, however, it is standard reading for law students when they embark on a course in constitutional law. It has influenced the development of jurisprudence in the American courts on the First Amendment to the US Constitution,[3] which guarantees freedom of the press as well as freedom of speech.

All is not doom and gloom, however, on this side of the Atlantic. We should not be embarrassed to remind ourselves from time to time of the contribution that Britain has made to the concept of human rights around the world for centuries.[4] It was after all at Runnymede that the first Magna Carta was signed in 1215.[5] Today, appropriately enough, there is also a monument to President Kennedy at the same site. Contrary to popular belief, this

---

[1] This essay is based on a lecture given to Young Justice on 2 May 1996.

[2] J Milton, *Areopagitica*, in *Complete English Poems, Of Education, Areopagitica* 4th edn (London, J.M. Dent & Sons, 1990) at 573–620.

[3] This provides that: "Congress shall make no law respecting an establishment of religion, or prohibiting the free exercise thereof; or abridging the freedom of speech, or of the press; or the right of the people peaceably to assemble, and to petition the Government for a redress of grievances."

[4] See Lord Bingham of Cornhill CJ, "The European Convention on Human Rights: Time to Incorporate" in R Gordon & R Wilmot-Smith (eds), *Human Rights in the United Kingdom* (Oxford, Clarendon Press, 1996) ch. 1.

[5] For a recent case in which the Court of Appeal referred to both the 1215 and the 1297 versions of Magna Carta, see *Re S-C (Mental Patient: Habeas Corpus)* [1996] QB 599 at 603C (Bingham MR).

country *does* have a bill of rights, the one dating from 1689.[6] Finally, it was British lawyers who were largely responsible for drafting the European Convention on Human Rights ("ECHR") after the end of World War II, and the United Kingdom was the first member of the Council of Europe to ratify that Convention.[7]

The common law also has, over the centuries, been capable of sensitivity to what in modern parlance would be called human rights. Take these words, for example, from the judgment of Lord Camden, the Chief Justice of the Common Pleas, in *Entick* v. *Carrington* – the classic case on search and seizure:

> "The great end, for which men entered into society, was to secure their property. That right is preserved sacred and incommunicable in all instances, where it has not been taken away or abridged by some public law for the good of the whole."[8]

The language in that passage reflects almost verbatim the words of John Locke.[9] Although that passage focuses on property rights, earlier in the same judgment Lord Camden said this:

> "[I]f this point should be determined in favour of the jurisdiction, the secret cabinets and bureaus of every subject in this Kingdom will be thrown open to the search and inspection of a messenger, whenever the secretary of state shall think fit to charge, or even to suspect, a person to be the author, printer, or publisher of a seditious libel."[10]

That is, in all but name, recognition of privacy as a value in the common law.[11] In *Entick* v. *Carrington*, the Secretary of State invoked an argument based on what he called "state necessity", something which politicians in all ages will resort to, although they may call it different things today, such as "national security" or "the prevention of terrorism". Lord Camden's response was this:

> ". . . and with respect to the argument of state necessity, or a distinction that has been aimed at between state offences and others, the common law does not under-

---

[6] The Bill of Rights does not set out the catalogue of rights that we have come to expect in the last two centuries and is primarily concerned with establishing the supremacy of Parliament over the Crown. However, it does contain some of the seeds of the rights which have flourished in later charters: for example, Article 10 prohibits "cruel and unusual punishments", a phrase which is directly found in the Eighth Amendment to the US Constitution and which finds a more distant echo in Article 3 of the European Convention on Human Rights.

[7] See A Lester QC, "Fundamental Rights: the United Kingdom Isolated?" [1984] PL 46; G Marston, "The United Kingdom's Part in the Preparation of the European Convention on Human Rights, 1950" (1993) 42 ICLQ 796.

[8] (1765) 19 State Trials 1029 at 1066.

[9] J. Locke, *Second Treatise of Civil Government* (London, Dent, 1970) ch. VIII.

[10] (1765) 19 State Trials 1029 at 1063.

[11] Contrast the view of L Lustgarten and I Leigh, *In From the Cold: National Security and Parliamentary Democracy* (Oxford, Clarendon Press, 1994) at 41–2, where it is suggested that the common law approach as exemplified in *Entick* v. *Carrington* is essentially based on the concept of property, rather than privacy.

stand that kind of reasoning, nor do our books take notice of any such distinction."[12]

I would suggest that it is possible for us to reclaim that heritage, common not only to the Anglo-American legal world but to the world as a whole in the late twentieth century, and to speak again the language of liberty.[13]

Indeed, many of the legal concepts familiar to public lawyers in this country are *already* based upon notions that would be described as human rights elsewhere in the world. For example, it is elementary that, before a public decision-maker deprives somebody of property or some other interest pursuant to a discretionary power, the courts will imply into the statutory framework the requirements of "natural justice". In particular they will require that the decision-maker should not be biased and should afford the person affected a fair hearing before taking the decision in question.[14] Those requirements are not substantially different from what courts in other countries would require decision-makers to do, pursuant to a constitutional guarantee that no one shall be deprived of life, liberty or property without "due process of law".[15]

A second way in which public law, even on a traditional view, protects human rights is through the techniques of statutory interpretation. It is received wisdom that the supervisory jurisdiction of the High Court is based on the doctrine of *ultra vires*,[16] that is the principle that a public body may not exceed the powers which it is given by law, usually by legislation. Accordingly, the task for the court is often to ascertain the true meaning of a piece of legislation, which is said to confer a relevant power upon a public body to see if it does indeed do so. The approach of the court for a long time has been to interpret legislation by reference to certain presumptions of statutory construction. One of those presumptions is that Parliament should not lightly be taken to have intended to interfere with, or permit the executive to interfere with, certain "basic" or "constitutional" rights of the individual.[17] A famous example is provided by *R v. Secretary of State for the Home Department, ex parte Leech*,[18] where the Court of Appeal recognised a constitutional right of access to the courts.

---

[12] (1765) 19 State Trials 1029 at 1073.

[13] See, for a survey of a period when the Anglo-American world had a common language of liberty, JCD Clark, *The Language of Liberty 1660–1832* (Cambridge, Cambridge University Press, 1994).

[14] See, for example, S.A. de Smith, Lord Woolf & J. Jowell, *Judicial Review of Administrative Action* 5th edn (London, Sweet and Maxwell, 1995) chs 7–10; *R v. Secretary of State for the Home Department, ex p. Fayed* [1997] 1 All ER 228 at 237j–238b (Lord Woolf MR) and 251c–f (Phillips LJ).

[15] See, for example, the Fifth and Fourteenth Amendments to the US Constitution.

[16] See the extra-judicial view of Sir John Laws, "Illegality: The Problem of Jurisdiction" in M. Supperstone & J. Goudie (eds) *Judicial Review* (London, Butterworth, 1992) ch. 4 especially at 52–4 and 67–8; and also D Oliver, "Is the ultra vires rule the basis of judicial review?" [1987] PL 543; C Forsyth, "Of Fig Leaves and Fairy Tales . . ." (1996) 55 CLJ 122.

[17] See, for example, *Halsbury's Laws of England* 4th edn reissue, (London, Butterworth, 1995) Vol. 44(1), paras 1455–68.

[18] [1994] QB 198 at 210 (Steyn LJ, as he then was).

A recent interesting example of this technique of statutory interpretation is provided by the decision of the Divisional Court in *R* v. *Lord Chancellor, ex p. Witham*.[19] The applicant in that case sought a declaration that Article 3 of the Supreme Court Fees (Amendment) Order 1996 was *ultra vires* section 130 of the Supreme Court Act 1981. Article 3 repealed certain provisions in the Supreme Court Fees Order 1980, which relieved litigants in person who were in receipt of income support from the obligation to pay court fees, for example for issuing a writ. The fee for issuing a writ was increased in some cases to £500. This had the effect, on evidence which the Court accepted,[20] of preventing people on low incomes from starting court proceedings and from taking certain steps in defending proceedings that others had begun against them (such as possession proceedings which can deprive someone of their home). In the main judgment (with which Rose LJ agreed) Laws J set out an eloquent analysis of the concept of "constitutional rights" in a system such as the British one:

"The common law does not generally speak in the language of constitutional rights, for the good reason that in the absence of a sovereign text, a written constitution which is logically and legallly prior to the power of legislature, executive and judiciary alike, there is on the face of it no hierarchy of rights such that any one of them is more entrenched by law than any other . . . In the unwritten legal order of the British State, at a time when the common law continues to accord a legislative supremacy to Parliament, the notion of a constitutional right can in my judgment inhere only in this proposition, that the right in question cannot be abrogated by the State save by specific provision in an Act of Parliament, or by regulations whose *vires* in main legislation specifically confers the power to abrogate. General words will not suffice. And any such rights will be the creature of the common law, since their existence would not be the consequence of the democratic political process but would be logically prior to it."[21]

Laws J turned to apply the above principle to the facts of the case before the Court and held:

"Access to the courts is a constitutional right; it can only be denied by the government if it persuades Parliament to pass legislation which specifically – in effect by express provision – permits the executive to turn people away from the court door. That has not been done in this case."

The Court accordingly decided that the Lord Chancellor had no *vires* to make Article 3 of the 1996 Order since Parliament had not expressly authorised him to make an order which would have the effect of denying access to the courts to people on very low incomes.[22]

---

[19] [1997] 2 All ER 779.

[20] On the use of evidence of this type (which was put in by the Public Law Project, a public interest organisation) see *infra* Chapter 7.

[21] At 783f–784a.

[22] Although the decision is welcome in its express recognition of the concept of constitutional rights in the common law, it is, in my view, regrettable that the judgment of Laws J draws a distinction between the negative and positive aspects of the duty on the state that the concept of a constitutional right imposes. I return to this distinction in more detail in Chapter 3 *infra*.

There is nothing new in this approach. The courts have long been careful to construe powers to make delegated legislation in a narrow way, so as to avoid what I would describe as violation of fundamental constitutional principles. For example, in *Attorney General* v. *Wiltshire United Dairies Ltd*[23] the Court of Appeal held that a power to make regulations for the defence of the realm and thereby to regulate the supply of milk did not confer power on the executive to impose taxes upon the subject without authorisation from Parliament. That would be contrary to the principle reflected in Article 4 of the Bill of Rights 1689.

What is relatively new is that the common law has started to move away from its traditional concentration on personal liberty and property rights. Courts have increasingly been prepared to recognise, both expressly and impliedly, the existence of certain other fundamental rights, such as freedom of expression and the right to respect for private life: see, for example, *R* v. *Secretary of State for the Home Department, ex p. Brind*,[24] which concerned the ban on broadcasting the voices of Sinn Fein supporters, and *R* v. *Ministry of Defence, ex p. Smith*[25] which concerned the compulsory discharge of homosexuals from the Armed Forces. Furthermore, in many cases, the courts have not felt it necessary to make direct reference to any international treaty on human rights in order to achieve that result. Even when they have referred, for example, to the ECHR, they have often done so merely by way of reinforcing the conclusion to which they would have come in any event as to the position at common law: see, for example, the approach of Lord Templeman to freedom of expression in *Brind* itself. The same approach permeates the case of *Derbyshire County Council* v. *Times Newspapers Ltd*,[26] which is a private law case in form, but which reflects an important recognition of the place of human rights concepts in the common law. There the House of Lords held that a local authority may not sue for defamation, because of the chilling effect such a cause of action would have on the freedom of the press to criticise public bodies in a democracy.

Moreover, our courts have come expressly to recognise that there are certain values inherent in the common law which may be termed "fundamental" – such interests or rights are to be distinguished from those rights which are recognised by the law but are not accorded the same pre-eminent status.[27]

The interesting aspect of this recent development is that the common law may at last be setting itself free from the constraints of an approach to human rights which might otherwise have fossilised in 1689. In particular the common law is beginning to recognise that human beings have fundamental needs which are not regarded in traditional liberal thought as being fundamental

---

[23] (1921) 19 LGR 534.
[24] [1991] 1 AC 696.
[25] [1996] QB 517.
[26] [1993] AC 534.
[27] See, for example, *R* v. *Secretary of State for the Home Department, ex p. McQuillan* [1995] 4 All ER 400, at 421–2 (Sedley J); *R* v. *Lord Chancellor, ex p. Witham* [1997] 2 All ER 779 (DC).

rights, for example the need for shelter with a modicum of security.[28] I would suggest that more of these "second generation" rights, as they are called in international law, may come to be recognised as being of fundamental importance in the common law, such as the right to adequate health care.[29] In this way, the common law can evolve in step with the needs of a modern society.

What then is the consequence of the courts' recognition of an interest as a fundamental right or need? This question arises in particular in the context of what may be on the face of it a very broad discretionary power conferred by statute upon a public body. In a particular case that power may be exercised in a way which interferes with what the court recognises as a fundamental right or need. Traditionally, public law would be unable to quash the decision simply on the ground that it interfered with such a right or need. On the present state of the authorities,[30] the following seven propositions seem to be established:

(1) Even without enactment of a human rights instrument such as the ECHR into domestic law, the courts recognise that there are certain fundamental rights which enjoy a pre-eminent status within the common law. These include the right to life, freedom of expression, freedom of movement and the right to respect for private and family life.

(2) The court will require the public body concerned to take the relevant right into account.

(3) The court will require that public body to balance the impact of the decision concerned on the fundamental right against whatever public interests militate in favour of making that decision.

(4) The primary judgment as to whether that balance has been struck in the right place is for the public body on whom the power has been conferred. However, the court will perform a secondary judgment to assess the rationality of the decision taken.

(5) In assessing the rationality of the decision, the court will require greater justification (by way of countervailing public interests) for the decision taken, depending on the importance of the fundamental right affected and the breadth or gravity of the interference with that right.

---

[28] See *R* v. *Lincolnshire County Council, ex p. Atkinson* Times Law Reports, 22 September 1995 (Sedley J); *R* v. *Kerrier District Council, ex p. Uzell* (1996) 71 P & CR 566 (Latham J); *R* v. *Secretary of State for Social Security, ex p. JCWI* [1997] 1 WLR 275 (CA); *R* v. *Hammersmith and Fulham LBC, ex p. MAP and X* [1997] COD 140 (Collins J); Times Law Reports, 19 February 1997 (CA).

[29] In *R* v. *Secretary of State for the Home Department, ex p. Zakrocki*, Times Law Reports, 3 April 1996 (Carnwath J) arguments were put to the court on this basis but, since the court decided in favour of the applicant on other grounds, it did not need to go into those arguments, although it acknowledged that they might be important in other cases.

[30] See, in particular, *Bugdaycay* v. *Secretary of State for the Home Department* [1987] AC 514; *R* v. *Secretary of State for the Home Department, ex p. Brind* [1991] 1 AC 696; *R* v. *Ministry of Defence, ex p. Smith* [1996] QB 517 (CA); *R* v. *Secretary of State for the Home Department, ex p. McQuillan* [1995] 4 All ER 400 (Sedley J); *R* v. *Secretary of State for the Home Department, ex p. Zighem* [1996] Imm AR 194 (Latham J).

(6) The court will not be satisfied with a simple incantation of a ritual mantra, to the effect that the public body has taken into account the fundamental right at stake. The court will scrutinise the decision closely, sometimes most anxiously, in particular where the right to life is at stake.

(7) The court is unlikely to take a benevolent view of any defect in the decision-making process, for example by refusing relief in its discretion, as it might do if the case did not involve human rights.[31]

In the absence of such an exercise which can be clearly demonstrated to have taken place, the court will not be satisfied that due sensitivity has been shown to the fundamental interest at stake and indeed would be disabled from forming its own secondary judgment as to the rationality of the decision taken. Some authority for my sixth proposition comes from the recent judgment of Latham J in *R* v. *Secretary of State for the Home Department, ex p. Zighem*[32] where the Secretary of State in an immigration case had stated that he had taken into account Article 8 of the ECHR, which for present purposes guarantees the right to respect for family life. Nevertheless the court quashed the decision because it was not persuaded that the reasoning process as to the human rights issue in the case sufficiently demonstrated that the right questions had been asked.

Some may detect in some of my propositions what is implicitly a doctrine of proportionality. This is indeed the doctrine which dare not speak its name in English law. As Sedley J remarked in *R.* v. *Secretary of State for the Home Department, ex p. McQuillan*,[33] if the above approach does amount to recognition of a doctrine of proportionality in English public law, it does no more than what the House of Lords has contemplated with equanimity for some years now, in a series of cases starting with *Bugdaycay* v. *Secretary of State for the Home Department*.[34] Moreover, whatever the *ratio* of *Brind* may be, which is a vexed question, there is now Court of Appeal authority, approving what the Master of the Rolls in *Smith* called an "accurate distillation of the principles" which was formulated by David Pannick QC as follows:

"The court may not interfere with the exercise of administrative discretion on substantive grounds save where the court is satisfied that the decision is unreasonable in the sense that it is beyond the range of responses open to a reasonable decision-maker. But in judging whether the decision-maker has exceeded this margin of appreciation the human rights context is important. The more substantial the interference with human rights, the more the court will require by way of justification before it is satisfied that the decision is reasonable in the sense outlined above."[35]

[31] See *R* v. *Ministry of Defence, ex p. Smith* [1996] QB 517 at 537H–538B (Simon Brown LJ, when the case was in the Divisional Court).

[32] [1996] Imm AR 194 (Latham J).

[33] [1995] 4 All ER 400 at 423a.

[34] [1987] AC 514.

[35] [1996] QB 517 at 554E–F (Bingham MR); see also Henry LJ at 563A and Thorpe LJ at 565A.

In *R* v. *Chief Constable of Sussex, ex p. International Traders Ferry Ltd.*[36] Kennedy LJ acknowledged that, in the light of *Brind*, the concept of irrationality is different from that of proportionality[37] and cited a lecture in which Lord Hoffmann had suggested that in many instances it is impossible to see daylight between the two concepts.[38] In any event, the express reasoning of the Court of Appeal in *Smith* and the outcome of the case itself suggest that the court is not entitled to assess a decision against the test of proportionality, only to ask whether it was open to a reasonable decision-maker to reach it, even if it *prima facie* violates a fundamental human right.

Before I move on, I should confess that, unlike some people, I do not regard the ability of the common law to protect human rights as ideal. The trouble with the common law is that it recognises liberty only as a "negative" idea: I am free to do whatever is not prohibited by some rule of law. Furthermore, it is axiomatic in our constitution that the common law is vulnerable to Act of Parliament. These two features of our system came together graphically in the recent case of *DPP* v. *Jones*.[39] In that case an order had been obtained by the police from the local authority banning "trespassory assemblies" within a four-mile radius of Stonehenge for a period of four days. Such an order, which can be obtained on the grounds set out in section 14A of the Public Order Act 1986, as amended by the Criminal Justice and Public Order Act 1994, applies to assemblies of twenty or more persons,[40] and prohibits any such assembly which is held on land to which the public has no access or only limited access and takes place without the permission of the occupier or so as to exceed the limits of any permission or "the limits of the public's right of access".[41] A person who takes part in an assembly which he knows is prohibited under section 14A is guilty of an offence.[42] The respondents in the case were defendants who had taken part in an assembly on a grass verge near Stonehenge. It was agreed as a matter of fact between the parties that the assembly was peaceful; that it did not cause an obstruction of the highway; and that it was not considered by the police to be a public nuisance.

In principle it would be possible for the common law to recognise that the "public's right of access" to land which is *publicly* owned, namely the highway, includes the right to demonstrate,[43] but there were numerous authorities against that view and the Divisional Court held that the respondents' convictions had to be restored. Moreover, it was not open to the respondents to

---

[36] [1997] 2 All ER 65 (CA).

[37] I come back to this distinction at greater length *infra* Chapter 3.

[38] Lord Hoffmann, "A Sense of Proportion" (unpublished lecture, 14 November 1996), referred to in *R* v. *Chief Constable of West Sussex, ex p. ITF Ltd* [1997] 2 All ER 65 at 80h.

[39] [1997] 2 All ER 119 (DC).

[40] Section 14A(9) of the Public Order Act 1986.

[41] Section 14A(5) of the Public Order Act 1986.

[42] Section 14B(2) of the Public Order Act 1986.

[43] For an outline of US constitutional law on the doctrine of the "public forum", which includes streets and parks, where First Amendment rights of speech and assembly are protected, see *infra* Chapter 4.

argue that the circumstances in which an order can be obtained under section 14A are themselves inconsistent with the right to freedom of assembly; or that the procedural protections that a due respect for that right would entail are absent from the scheme of section 14A. The decision to make orders banning trespassory assemblies is one vested in branches of the executive alone (including the police), without any judicial intervention. The net result of the case is to confirm that freedom of assembly is not regarded in the common law as being even as important as passing and repassing along the highway (in modern parlance, driving or walking up and down the road), let alone of fundamental importance in our legal system.[44]

There are two important problems, not only of law but also of politics, which the new human rights approach to public law raises for our society.

First is the question of sources – where do these fundamental rights or needs come from? Are they simply reflections of the ideological preferences of each individual judge who sits in the Crown Office List of the Queen's Bench Division? To adapt the phrase of the American judge, Oliver Wendell Holmes,[45] if the economic theories of Herbert Spencer are not part of the common law, neither are those of Karl Marx. But how are the judges to know which rights and needs are fundamental? One suggestion that has been made is that they should only regard those rights as fundamental which are "accepted values of our democratic society . . . values that no democratic politician, consistently with his status as such, could be heard to deny".[46] I take it that what is meant by a "democratic society" in this context is, as the European Court of Human Rights has put it, one which is characterised by "pluralism, tolerance and broadmindedness".[47] In that sense, respect for fundamental rights, including the right to be different or unconventional, is an aspect of democracy. However, some people think of democracy as being the same as whatever the majority think at a given time. If this concept is to be a source of human rights, it suffers from both a practical problem and a problem of principle. The practical problem is that it is not obvious how judges are to discover what is "accepted" in our society. Are they to conduct, or to receive evidence of, opinion polls?

[44] In an admittedly *obiter* passage (at 127h–j) Collins J suggested that the result in *Jones* was consistent with the ECHR since the European Commission of Human Rights had recognised, in *Rassemblement Jurassien* v. *Switzerland* (App No 8191/78) (1979) 17 DR 93 at 119, that conditions such as authorisation may be imposed on the holding of assemblies on the highway. I would respectfully respond that while, as I observe *infra* in Chapter 4, reasonable time, place and manner regulations of assemblies are consistent with freedom of assembly and freedom of expression, it is difficult to see how an assembly that is peaceful and does not cause an obstruction or a public nuisance can be *totally* banned (not just regulated) within a wide area consistently with the requirement that interference with such rights should be "necessary in a democratic society".
[45] *Lochner* v. *New York* 198 US 45 (1905) at 75.
[46] Lord Irvine of Lairg QC, "Judges and Decision-Makers: The Theory and Practice of *Wednesbury* Review" [1996] PL 59 at 65. The author is now the Lord Chancellor in the new Labour government elected in 1997, which is committed to incorporating the European Convention on Human Rights into domestic law.
[47] *Handyside* v. *United Kingdom*, Series A, No. 24 (1979–80) 1 EHRR 737, para. 49.

The problem of principle is perhaps more important. In America too it used to be said that the courts should find implied rights in the Constitution only if they were rooted in American traditions.[48] However, as the political commentator Garry Wills once pointed out, it is as much an American tradition to run people out of town as it is to declare their rights.[49]

If the values which are fundamental are those which are accepted by the majority, perhaps the vast majority, of people, they are unlikely to be formulated in such a way as to protect the very people who need protection – unpopular minorities who may have no vote or who may be ineffective in exercising power through the ballot box. Take the controversial question of whether people's sexual orientation is essentially a private matter for them, not for others nor for the state. If the letters pages of the *Daily Mail* or even *The Times* are to be a guide to what are accepted values in our society, it is unlikely that that freedom will emerge as such a value. I would suggest that better sources of human rights would be the following four.

First, the common law itself. The common law, as we have seen from the passages quoted from *Entick* v. *Carrington*, contains within it rich seams reflecting the values it holds most dear – seams which modern judges can re-open and mine. This approach has the virtue that the enthusiasm of any one judge to discover new rights will be constrained by traditional common law reasoning, including development on a case-by-case basis.[50]

The second possible source is fundamental rights legislation. This is not a phrase which is often heard in Britain. Nevertheless I would suggest that Parliament has over the centuries announced certain values or norms which have become fundamental to the British system of government, even though (and sometimes because) they were not recognised as such at common law. Historical examples would include the Bill of Rights 1689. More recently the various Reform Acts which eventually established the principle of universal adult suffrage in 1928 have surely created a right which is basic to our democratic system: the right to vote. In the last three decades, Parliament has established the principle of equality, at least in the sense that discrimination on grounds such as race, sex and disability have been prohibited. At common law, there was no prohibition against racial discrimination although liberal judges tried to use other doctrines to fill the gap at least in part: see *Constantine* v. *Imperial Hotels Ltd.*[51] Yet the prohibition of discrimination on at least these three grounds must surely have become so self-evidently a fun-

---

[48] See, for example, *Griswold* v. *Connecticutt* 381 US 479 (1965), at 487 (Goldberg J., concurring).

[49] G Wills, quoted in J H Ely, *Democracy and Distrust* (Cambridge, Massachusetts, Harvard University Press) at 60.

[50] See Lord Steyn, "The Weakest and Least Dangerous Department of Government" [1997] PL 84 at 85.

[51] [1944] KB 693 (Birkett J). In that case it was held that the common law duty of an innkeeper to offer accommodation to travellers was breached when the plaintiff (the famous West Indian cricketer) was refused hotel accommodation on the ground of his race.

damental principle that today it is inconceivable that a discriminatory policy would withstand judicial review proceedings on the ground of *Wednesbury* unreasonableness.[52] Similarly, the impact of legislation on equality between the sexes has become so pervasive that it is easy to forget that the common law was riddled with discrimination against women.[53]

The third possible source is customary international law. A much neglected doctrine of English law is that customary international law, unlike the sort of international law that is found in treaties, is part of the common law – it does not need incorporation (or, as international lawyers strictly call it, "transformation") by Act of Parliament. This doctrine goes back at least to the middle of the eighteenth century: see *Triquet* v. *Bath*.[54] It was put perhaps most famously by Lord Atkin in *Chung Chi Cheung* v. *The King*:

> "The courts acknowledge the existence of a body of rules which nations accept among themselves. On any judicial issue they seek to ascertain what the relevant rule is, and, having found it, they will treat it as incorporated into the domestic law, so far as it is not inconsistent with rules enacted by statutes or finally declared by their tribunals."[55]

But what is customary international law depends on what is called "state practice". And state practice is often evidenced by what states around the world have accepted as their obligations in *treaties or in resolutions* of international organisations such as the United Nations. Thus, it would not be difficult to argue that customary international law today prohibits torture and racial discrimination, both of which are prohibited by multilateral treaties sponsored by the United Nations, whereas not so long ago both were openly practised even by countries in the West.[56]

The fourth possible source is European Community ("EC") law. Where there is a specific provision in the EC Treaty, in a regulation or in a directive, which has direct effect – so that it confers rights enforceable in a national court – there is no difficulty. An English court is required by EC law to

---

[52] See, for example, *R* v. *Ethical Committee of St. Mary's Hospital (Manchester), ex p. Harriott* [1988] 2 FLR 512 at 518H–519A (Schiemann J, *obiter*); and the prescient judgment of Scarman LJ (as he then was) dissenting in *Ahmad* v. *ILEA* [1978] QB 36 at 48C–D.

[53] See generally K O' Donovan, *Sexual Divisions in Law* (London, Weidenfeld & Nicholson, 1985) especially chs 1–2. It is widely accepted that the common law today would not tolerate sex discrimination since the right of both sexes to equal treatment can be regarded as one of the "unalienable rights" which the common law recognises. See S Kentridge QC's 1996 Harry Street Lecture: "Parliamentary Supremacy and the Judiciary under a Bill of Rights: Some Lessons from the Commonwealth" [1997] PL 96 at 97.

[54] (1764) 3 Burr. 1478 (Lord Mansfield, the Chief Justice of the King's Bench).

[55] [1937] AC 160 at 168 (PC).

[56] For more detailed expositions of the possible use of customary international law in domestic law, see M Hunt, *Using Human Rights Law in English Courts* (Oxford, Hart Publishing, 1997) at 11–13 and 20–31; A Drzemczewski, "The Applicability of Customary International Human Rights Law in the English Legal System" (1975) 8 HRJ 71; AJ Cunningham, "The European Convention on Human Rights, Customary International Law and the Constitution" (1994) 43 ICLQ 537; T Meron, *Human Rights and Humanitarian Norms as Customary Law* (Oxford, Clarendon Press, 1989) especially ch. II.

protect the right in question.[57] What I have in mind is situations where there is no directly effective right in play, perhaps because there is no European element in the case at all. Even then, EC law may provide the inspiration for development of the common law. For example, the principle of equality is one of the general principles of EC law. It is reflected in specific instruments such as the Equal Treatment Directive[58] but is not confined to them, as the Advocate-General and the European Court of Justice have recently reminded us in the case about discrimination against transsexuals, *P v. S and Cornwall County Council*.[59] A general principle of equality may well find its way into English public law over the next few years – it is up to innovative lawyers to make such arguments encouraged by what has been called the "gradual convergence" of European law and national legal systems in the European Union.[60]

So much for the problem of the sources of human rights. The other problem which arises is that of democracy or legitimacy. If the judges continue to find fundamental rights or needs buried deep within the common law, are they simply legislating human rights treaties into English law without the authority of Parliament? What I am calling for is not judicial incorporation of treaties by the back door, or the front door. I do suggest – as was put to me by a judge in the Crown Office List recently – that the courts can "look through the window" and look to human rights norms around the world, just as they would look at the judgments of foreign courts or at academic writings, so as to inform themselves as to the content of the common law. In this I am only following where others, most notably Sir John Laws, have led.[61]

However, I would acknowledge that the *preferable* route for this country to take in the longer term is for Parliament to enact a Bill of Rights, perhaps put to the people in a referendum.[62] That way, the problems I have identified – of sources of human rights and of democracy and legitimacy – should be avoided. However, in the absence of parliamentary will, the courts should continue to develop the common law in such a way as to protect human rights in public law. By so doing, they have woken the common law from its long slumber; they have started to reclaim their human rights heritage and to refine it so as to meet the needs of late twentieth-century society.

[57] See section 2(1) of the European Communities Act 1972 and authorities such as *R v. Secretary of State for Transport, ex p. Factortame Ltd* [1990] 2 AC 85 at 143 (Lord Bridge) and *R v. Secretary of State for Transport, ex p. Factortame Ltd (No 2)* [1991] 1 AC 603 at 658 (Lord Bridge). See also Hunt *supra* n. 55, at 52–63.

[58] Directive 76/207/EEC.

[59] Case C–13/94 [1996] ICR 795 (ECJ).

[60] B Markesinis (ed.), *The Gradual Convergence: Foreign Ideas, Foreign Influences, and English Law on the Eve of the 21st Century* (Oxford, Clarendon Press, 1994).

[61] See, for example, Sir John Laws, "Is the High Court the Guardian of Fundamental Constitutional Rights?" [1993] PL 59.

[62] In Chapter 2 *infra* I consider some of the issues that would arise if incorporation of the European Convention on Human Rights took place.

2

How to Incorporate the European Convention on Human Rights

INTRODUCTION

In Chapter 1, I mentioned that my preference is for a Bill of Rights to be enacted by Parliament. This would give democratic legitimacy to the efforts being tentatively made by some British judges to develop human rights in the common law. It would give the judges a clear idea of which rights are to be treated as fundamental in our society. It would also serve the function which all charters through the ages have performed – of giving a concrete form to the rights of the people, something to which they can point whenever a dispute about their rights arises. In this way, one of the most important functions of a Bill of Rights can be an educational one.[1] It would also have enormous beneficial impact in changing the legal culture of the United Kingdom, because legal education (for practitioners as well as for students) would have to take it seriously, as happened, albeit slowly, after European Community ("EC") law became part of the law of this country.

The arguments in favour of enacting a Bill of Rights have been put elegantly and cogently by others.[2] While the arguments against enacting a Bill of Rights are serious ones, I myself do not find them persuasive. The most important argument is the one based on democracy, which suggests that there is something illegitimate about the judicial enforcement of human rights.[3] Elsewhere in this book, I suggest that there is no dichotomy between democracy and human rights: that in fact they are symbiotic.[4]

In this chapter, therefore, I would like to look at the mechanics of enacting a Bill of Rights, for, if it is to be done at all, it should be done properly, because the chance to get it right may not come again. The new Labour government, which was elected in May 1997, is committed to incorporation of

---

[1] See F Klug, "Human Rights as Secular Ethics" in R Gordon & R Wilmot-Smith (eds), *Human Rights in the United Kingdom* (Oxford, Clarendon Press, 1996), ch. 5.

[2] See, for example, Lord Bingham of Cornhill CJ, "The European Convention on Human Rights: Time to Incorporate" in Gordon & Wilmot-Smith (eds) *supra* n. 1, ch. 1; M Zander, *A Bill of Rights?* 4th edn, (London, Sweet & Maxwell, 1997); R Dworkin, *Freedom's Law* (Oxford, OUP, 1996) ch. 18.

[3] See, for example, K D Ewing & C A Gearty, "Rocky Foundations for Labour's New Rights" [1997] EHRLR 146 especially at 148.

[4] See *infra* Chapter 3.

the European Convention on Human Rights ("ECHR") and a Bill to achieve this was announced in its first Queen's Speech. Not only does the Labour Party have a huge majority over all other parties in the House of Commons but it has agreed a joint programme of constitutional reform with the Liberal Democrats, so the majority in favour of incorporation is even larger.

In theory, it would be possible to enact a wholly new Bill of Rights. This may be desirable in the long term but experience from countries such as Canada and South Africa suggests that the process of drafting a new Bill of Rights is rightly time-consuming, since it requires a lengthy nationwide discussion in order to give it legitimacy and popular support.[5] Nor is it obvious that the best of the "off the shelf" models on offer is the ECHR. It would be possible to incorporate an international treaty other than the ECHR. In the case of Hong Kong, for example, the British Government incorporated the 1966 International Covenant on Civil and Political Rights.[6] There are sound reasons in principle for doing this. For example, the ECHR is notorious for the absence from it of a freestanding right to equality.[7] Article 14 prohibits discrimination only in the enjoyment of the other rights found elsewhere in the ECHR: very often the Strasbourg institutions decline to give a ruling on a complaint under Article 14 on the ground that no separate issue is raised which has not already been considered under another provision of the ECHR. The International Covenant, on the other hand, contains a powerful general principle of equality in Article 26, which provides that:

> ". . . the law shall prohibit *any* discrimination and guarantee to all persons equal and effective protection against discrimination *on any ground such as* race, colour, sex, language, religion, political or other opinion, national or social origin, property, birth *or other status.*" (*emphasis added*)

However, the easiest and most likely way to enact a domestic Bill of Rights at least in the short term is to incorporate the ECHR.[8] There is a high degree of consensus about this. This is probably because the United Kingdom already recognises the right of individual petition to the European Commission of Human Rights[9] and it is difficult to argue against the proposition that, if individuals are entitled to bring complaints before judges in Strasbourg, they should be able to bring them in the UK (at less expense and with less delay).

---

[5] B McLachlin, "The Canadian Charter and the Democratic Process" in C Gearty & A Tomkins (eds), *Understanding Human Rights* (London, Mansell, 1996) ch. 2, especially at 24 (the author is a Justice of the Supreme Court of Canada); S Kentridge QC, "Parliamentary Supremacy and the Judiciary under a Bill of Rights: Some Lessons from the Commonwealth" [1997] PL 96 at 100–101.

[6] See the Hong Kong Bill of Rights Ordinance (Ordinance No.59 of 1991); R Swede, "One Territory – Three Systems? The Hong Kong Bill of Rights" (1995) 44 ICLQ 358.

[7] See further J Wadham, "Why Incorporation of the European Convention is not Enough" in Gordon & Wilmot-Smith *supra* n. 1 ch.4: the author is the Director of Liberty (the National Council for Civil Liberties).

[8] There is no reason why a Bill incorporating the ECHR could not also include Article 26 of the International Covenant, a position supported by many who wish to see incorporation as soon as possible.

[9] Under article 25 of the ECHR.

Incorporation of the ECHR is what the Labour Party's consultation paper "Bringing Rights Home" published in December 1996 proposes. It is also proposed by the Report of the Joint Consultative Committee on Constitutional Reform published by the Labour and Liberal Democrat Parties in March 1997.[10] That Report rightly observes that:

> "Incorporation of the ECHR would represent a very significant strengthening in practice of what amounts to the UK's fundamental law."[11]

The Contents of an Incorporation Act

Parliament will have to decide which parts of the ECHR it incorporates. Clearly some of the provisions are inappropriate for incorporation because they are addressed to Contracting States and operate in terms at the level of international law.[12] However, the substantive rights should be incorporated.[13] Most of these are to be found in the main Convention but some have been added in four protocols.[14]

The paper "Bringing Rights Home"[15] seems to treat the concept of non-ratification of an international treaty (or a protocol to it) and reservation to it as if they were synonymous. In fact, the government will have to decide two different questions. The first is whether the United Kingdom should ratify those protocols which it has not to date ratified, such as Protocol No. 4, which includes the right of nationals of a country to enter its territory. Parliament would then have to decide whether to enact those further rights into domestic law; this might be done at the same time as the main Incorporation Act or under a provision in it which would permit a minister such as the Lord Chancellor to bring other rights into force through an Order in Council. The

---

[10] At paras. 17–23.

[11] See para. 23.

[12] For example Article 1 and sections II to V. Section I contains the main substantive rights but, while Articles 2 to 12 can probably be incorporated directly, Articles 13 to 18 would require modification if they are incorporated because they are either directed to the Contracting States or (especially in the case of Article 14, the equality provision) are unsatisfactory.

[13] The main rights in the ECHR are the following: the right to life (Article 2); freedom from torture and inhuman or degrading treatment or punishment (Article 3); freedom from slavery and compulsory labour (Article 4); the rights to liberty and security of the person and to safeguards in criminal procedure (Article 5); the right to a fair hearing in the determination of civil rights and obligations (Article 6); freedom from retrospective criminal penalties (Article 7); the right to respect for private and family life (Article 8); freedom of thought, conscience and religion (Article 9); freedom of expression (Article 10); freedom of assembly and association (Article 11); the right to marry and to found a family (Article 12); the right to peaceful enjoyment of possessions (Article 1 of Protocol No.1).

[14] The other protocols have been concerned with procedure. Most importantly, Protocol No. 11 will radically reform the institutions and procedures in Strasbourg, notably by creating a new court instead of the present Commission and Court. See further R Ryssdall, "The Coming of Age of the European Convention on Human Rights" [1996] EHRLR 18.

[15] J. Straw and P. Boateng, "Bringing Rights Home: Labour's Plans to Incorporate the European Convention on Human Rights into UK Law" [1997] EHRLR 71 at 75.

other question is whether to remove any reservations that have been entered by the United Kingdom to provisions in the Convention and those protocols which it *has* ratified, pursuant to Article 64 of the Convention. These are not in the British Constitution a direct matter for Parliament, although it would be natural for this question to be addressed at the same time as this country is debating whether to incorporate the ECHR into domestic law.

THE PURPOSES OF INCORPORATION

It is important to bear in mind *why* incorporation is thought to be necessary, that is, what are the defects in current law which incorporation seeks to remedy? The main purpose of incorporation is to reduce the risk that rules or practices are allowed to go unchecked by national courts which ultimately are found to violate the ECHR in Strasbourg. Such violations are mainly brought about in the following ways:

(1) Rules of the common law may be incompatible with the ECHR. In situations where the common law is uncertain, the courts are now likely to try to align it with the ECHR, either directly or (which is much the same thing) by holding that the common law also protects fundamental rights.[16] This should prevent further occasions when it could be said that the position under the common law is different from that under the ECHR. However, it is still possible that "old" rules of the common law will from time to time be resurrected and place the United Kingdom in breach of its obligations under the ECHR. This is more theoretical than practical, since the House of Lords at least would probably overrule any such rule and, if it was based on a decision of the House itself, would use its power in the 1966 Practice Statement to depart from its own previous decisions.

(2) An Act of Parliament may violate the ECHR. It is a matter of debate how often this has actually been the cause of judgments against the United Kingdom in Strasbourg. It seems as if the number of occasions is rising.[17] Whether, and to what extent, incorporation would prevent this happening depends on what kind of shield of "entrenchment" protects the Incorporation Act. I return to this below.

(3) A piece of secondary legislation such as regulations made by a Minister of the Crown may violate the ECHR. Again, it is likely that the courts would try to prevent this even under existing law (*supra* Chapter 1). R

---

[16] See cases such as *Derbyshire County Council* v. *Times Newspapers Ltd* [1992] QB 770 (CA) and [1993] AC 534 (HL); and *supra* Chapter 1.

[17] See J Wadham, "Bringing Rights Half-way Home" [1997] EHRLR 141 at 143–5. Cf. Lord Lester of Herne Hill QC, when promoting his 1997 Bill to incorporate the ECHR: *Hansard* HL Deb, 5 February 1997, col 1728.

v. *Lord Chancellor, ex p. Witham*[18] is a recent example of this approach, even though the conclusion was expressly reached by the Divisional Court on the basis of the common law and without detailed consideration of the Strasbourg cases to which it was referred.

(4) An administrative discretion may be exercised without taking into account the fundamental rights affected. Again, it is unlikely in the modern state of the law, whatever *Brind*[19] may at one time have been thought to stand for, that a court in judicial review proceedings would find that this was lawful, even without incorporation.[20] It is likely today that a human right will be found to exist in the common law, and will be a relevant consideration which must be taken into account in the exercise of an administrative discretion. It may be desirable to put the matter beyond doubt, not least since no two counsel who appear in the Crown Office List can agree what *Brind* does stand for on this issue.

(5) A decision taken in the discretion of a public body may *prima facie* violate a fundamental right but may be justified by some countervailing public interest in circumstances where a court cannot regard the decision as irrational or *Wednesbury* unreasonable. As I will suggest (*infra* Chapter 3), this could well arise because the doctrine of proportionality which is required by the ECHR is not co-extensive with the English law doctrine of irrationality.[21] If this is the "*Brind* gap" it would be desirable to plug it. In practice, this is likely to be the most useful impact that incorporation would have on legal doctrine, at least in public law. We would do well to heed the words of the President of the European Court of Human Rights, Rolv Ryssdall, who has suggested that the effect of incorporation in the United Kingdom would enrich the ECHR system as a whole, because it would permit UK judges to determine issues under the ECHR directly. In a lecture in November 1995 he said:

> "Furthermore, for the cases that do reach Strasbourg, the Convention institutions will doubtless be heavily influenced by the decision of a *judicial body* that has carried out that balancing exercise having regard to the Convention and to the case law of its institutions. Where, as in many British cases, the applicant has not been able to plead before a domestic court on the same basis as under the Convention, the Strasbourg enforcement bodies are more likely to appear to be sitting as a court of first instance in relation to the Convention grievances. Hence the appearance of undertaking an assessment more appropriate for a *domestic court*. I agree: these are assessments which, in the first place, *national judges* are better placed to make, thereby allowing

---

[18] [1997] 2 All ER 779 (DC).

[19] *R* v. *Secretary of State for the Home Department, ex p. Brind* [1991] 1 AC 696.

[20] See *supra* Chapter 1; M J Beloff and H Mountfield, "Unconventional Behaviour? Judicial Uses of the European Convention in English Law" [1996] EHRLR 467; M Hunt, *Using Human Rights Law in English Courts* (Oxford, Hart Publishing, 1997) ch. 6.

[21] See also *R* v. *Ministry of Defence, ex p. Smith* [1996] QB 517; and S Kentridge QC, "Parliamentary Supremacy and the Judiciary Under a Bill of Rights: Some Lessons from the Commonwealth" [1997] PL 96 at 98–9.

the international judges to confine themselves to the more comfortable role of secondary review."[22]

(6) The way in which a *court* exercises a discretion may infringe a fundamental right in the ECHR, for example where an interlocutory injunction is granted restraining a publication in breach of the right to freedom of expression. Again, this is unlikely to happen today, since English courts try to exercise their own discretionary powers in accordance with fundamental human rights.[23]

The reason why it is important to be clear about what the aims of incorporation are is that, without a clear statement of the aims, it is difficult to choose the appropriate mechanism for incorporation. This is especially so since serious commentators on the subject such as Sir Nicholas Lyell (the former Attorney-General) are concerned about "the deceptively simple but crucial question: what do they [the proponents of incorporation] mean by incorporation?"[24] In my view, the answer in general terms is that incorporation of the ECHR would render it possible to rely on the rights set out in it in a national court or tribunal or, to adapt the parlance of EC law, those rights would have "direct effect". That is the objective: it provides the litmus test by which an Incorporation Act will be judged. The end result of incorporation should be that it should no longer be possible for a court in this country to hold that, although a rule of the common law, a legislative provision, or the exercise of an administrative or judicial discretion was in breach of the ECHR, it was powerless to do anything about it.

THE MECHANICS OF INCORPORATION

The next question is what form an Incorporation Act should take. In theory, it could be a one-clause Bill enacting the ECHR into domestic law, perhaps with a schedule setting out the text of the provisions intended to be so incorporated. However, incorporation may not be so easy. There are difficult issues that will at some stage need to be addressed relating to the scope and applicability of the Incorporation Act. These may be thought to be too difficult to address in the Incorporation Act itself. However, it would be as well to antic-

---

[22] R Ryssdall, "The Coming of Age of the European Convention on Human Rights" [1996] EHRLR 18 at 27 (*emphasis added*).

[23] See, for example, *R* v. *Advertising Standards Authority, ex p. Vernons Organisation Ltd* [1992] 1 WLR 1289 (Laws J). Cf. the interlocutory injunction that was granted in the "Spycatcher" litigation: *Attorney-General* v. *Guardian* [1987] 1 WLR 1248 (HL); and what happened in Strasbourg when the litigation reached there: *Observer and Guardian* v. *United Kingdom* Series A, No. 216 (1992) 14 EHRR 153; *Sunday Times* v. *United Kingdom (No 2)* Series A, No. 217 (1992) 14 EHRR 229.

[24] Sir Nicholas Lyell QC, "Whither Strasbourg? Why Britain should think long and hard before incorporating the European Convention on Human Rights" [1997] EHRLR 132 at 137.

ipate as many of these as possible in advance and so give guidance to the courts in what will be for them largely uncharted territory. This is particularly true of the lower courts, which will probably form the "coalface" of human rights practice, as opposed to the higher courts, where the Law Lords have some experience of human rights cases by sitting in the Privy Council, which hears appeals from some Commonwealth countries that have written Constitutions and Bills of Rights.

Eligibility to Rely on the ECHR

In the ECHR system itself, the right of individual petition is conferred only on those who can claim to be "victims" of a violation of the rights contained in the ECHR.[25] This concept is similar to the concept of "standing" or *locus standi* which is found in most legal systems: it determines who can bring a complaint under the ECHR. However, since the ECHR provides a floor, not a ceiling, for the protection of human rights, it is open to the United Kingdom to adopt a wider concept of standing than the concept of "victim" would cover. In the last few years English public law has come to take a more generous attitude to the standing of groups that bring applications for judicial review not to vindicate their own legal rights but on behalf of others or in the public interest generally.[26] It would, therefore, be appropriate if the Act which incorporates the ECHR also recognised the concept of public interest standing. This suggestion is proposed by the paper "Bringing Rights Home"[27] and is to be welcomed. I would suggest that there may be a particular role in bringing test cases for a Human Rights Commission (see *infra*) but this should not preclude cases brought by non-governmental organisations. It is a feature of pluralist societies that the vigilance which is needed for the protection of human rights is never left entirely to the state itself: there is always a role for "civil society".[28]

A vexed question that arises is whether it should be open to limited companies and other bodies to bring cases under an Incorporation Act. The law refers to these as "legal" as opposed to "natural" persons. Of course, this is a fiction: they are not persons in the real sense and this has led some to suggest that they should not be able to claim the protection of an Act which is intended to confer *human* rights, since they are not human. In my view, this suggestion is wrong both on grounds of principle and on pragmatic grounds:

(1) The reason of principle is that some rights in human rights instruments are conferred on groups as well as individuals, for example, freedom of

---

[25] Article 25.1 of the ECHR.
[26] See further on this development *infra* Chapter 7.
[27] *Supra* n. 15 at 76.
[28] See further *infra* Chapter 7.

association and freedom of assembly.[29] It is true that it could be said that the right belongs only to the individual members of the group but this seems to be an artificial way of looking at the reality of the situation. In democratic societies, it is not only the members of a political party or trade union but the organisation itself that should be free to organise its internal affairs as it sees fit, subject to the general public interest.[30] Moreover, certain rights are expressly conferred by the ECHR on "legal" persons: for example the right to peaceful enjoyment of possessions, which is in essence a right to private property.[31] This right is by no means unqualified. Indeed, the wording of the right in the ECHR and the case-law on it permits a wider margin of appreciation to the state, in the fields of taxation and social protection of tenants from landlords for example, than most other provisions of the ECHR.[32] Nevertheless, the important point in this context is that, if the Incorporation Act were to deny protection to limited companies that wish to invoke the ECHR, that would in principle be a violation of the ECHR itself.[33] That would hardly be an auspicious start to the attempt to bring rights home.

(2) The reason based on pragmatic grounds derives from the fact that, very often, a human right will be invoked as a "shield" rather than a "sword" in legal proceedings. It may provide a defence to a civil action or criminal prosecution. It would be strange if an individual journalist or editor could raise it as a defence but at the same time the limited company which publishes the newspaper or magazine for which they work could not. Nor should it be thought that this would be of importance only to large companies owned by media moguls. In a notorious case in the late 1970s, it was not only the editor of *Gay News* but the company Gay News Limited that was prosecuted for blasphemy.[34] Likewise the company that publishes an article may be sued for defamation. In practice, the publication concerned could be put out of business if it has to pay a large fine (in criminal proceedings) or has to pay large damages, or has its assets sequestrated (in civil proceedings). It would

---

[29] See, for example, *Rassamblement Jurassien* v. *Switzerland* (App No. 8191/78) 17 DR 93 (1979); *Christians Against Racism and Fascism* v. *United Kingdom* (App No. 8840/78) 21 DR 138 (1980); *Plattform "Ärzte für das Leben"* v. *Austria* Series A, No. 139 (1991) 13 EHRR 204.

[30] See for an example from the case-law of the US Supreme Court: *NAACP* v. *Alabama* 357 US 449 (1958), where the famous civil rights organisation was permitted to assert the right to freedom of association of its members in the face of restrictive state laws.

[31] Article 1 of Protocol No. 1 to the ECHR.

[32] See, for example, *James* v. *United Kingdom* Series A, No. 98 (1986) 8 EHRR 123; and *Wasa Liv* v. *Sweden* (App No. 13013/87) 58 DR 163 (1988).

[33] See further Zander, *supra* n. 2, at 153–5. As well as being inconsistent with a provision such as Article 1 of Protocol No. 1, preventing a company from relying upon other provisions of the ECHR could be said to discriminate against them on the ground of their status in breach of Article 14.

[34] *R* v. *Lemon* [1979] AC 617.

also be ironic if, at a time when it is increasingly recognised that organisations should be able to bring court cases in the public interest and when such organisations are often (and may be required to be) limited companies,[35] they could not rely on an Incorporation Act.

I do appreciate the irritation which many people feel at the prospect of an Incorporation Act being "hi-jacked" by the rich and powerful to protect their interests against progressive action by the state. However, in my view, there are other ways of mitigating that risk, as I suggest in Chapter 3; the answer does not lie in denying the protection of human rights to companies altogether.

On Whom Should the Incorporation Act be Binding?

Should the Act bind everyone or only public bodies? In principle, there is a powerful case for saying that human rights should be protected against everyone, not just against the state. It is a rather old-fashioned liberal idea that rights are under threat only from the state. Even in the US Constitution, some rights are binding on everyone: the best example is the prohibition of slavery in the Thirteenth Amendment, which was absent from the original Bill of Rights and was passed only after the Civil War. Generally, however, the rights in the US Constitution require infringement by some "state action" before they can be invoked.[36] In English law, some fundamental rights are already protected against private individuals and companies, as in the case of the race relations and sex discrimination legislation.[37] However, again a pragmatic view may have to be taken: at first at least, since the ECHR is the model to be incorporated, and since the ECHR applies only to Contracting States, the Incorporation Act could and should bind only public bodies.[38]

If the Incorporation Act should be binding only on public bodies, how are such bodies to be defined?[39] Should the test used in EC law for the direct effect

---

[35] See *infra* Chapter 7.

[36] See, for example, *Barron* v. *Baltimore* 7 Pet (32 US) 243 (1833), in which the US Supreme Court held that the Bill of Rights did not bind the states but only the federal government; the *Civil Rights Cases* 109 US 3 (1883), in which the Court emasculated the first attempts by Congress to pass legislation prohibiting racial discrimination by private individuals and entities, an attempt which had to wait another eighty years before it was successful; and *Marsh* v. *Alabama* 326 US 501 (1946), in which the Court acknowledged that sometimes a private owner of land will have such a monopoly over the constitutional rights of individuals (that case concerned freedom of speech on sidewalks in a "company town") that state action will be implicated.

[37] Race Relations Act 1976; Sex Discrimination Act 1975.

[38] On the concept of "*Drittwirkung*" – what might be called in the parlance of EC law "horizontal direct effect" – see A Clapham, *Human Rights in the Private Sphere* (Oxford, Clarendon Press, 1993).

[39] The Labour Party's paper "Bringing Rights Home" *supra* n. 15 at 76 suggests that "it should apply only to public authorities – government departments, executive agencies, quangos, local authorities and other public services."

of directives (whether a body is an emanation of the state[40]) be adopted? The paper "Bringing Rights Home" says: "An appropriate definition would be included in the new legislation and this might be framed in terms of bodies performing public functions."[41] I agree with this but the test of "public functions" would need to be defined in some way. One way of providing a test would be to link the reach of the Incorporation Act to the tests developed by the courts at common law for deciding whether a body is amenable to an application for judicial review.[42]

One other problem may need express recognition. It should be made clear for the avoidance of doubt that the acts of an officer of a public body are to be treated as its acts, even if those acts exceed that person's lawful authority. This would be consistent with the approach in the USA, where an act which is done "under colour of law" is attributable to a public body even though it is clearly unlawful.[43]

The Labour Party's paper "Bringing Rights Home", says that:

"Individuals would in certain circumstances be able to use the new Act to seek to secure effective action by public authorities to protect them against abuse of human rights by private bodies or individuals. Nevertheless this new legislation is not intended to alter existing legal relationships between individuals."[44]

I agree with this but the "certain circumstances" need to be defined in some way. The case-law from Strasbourg would suggest that, while the obligations in the ECHR are imposed on the state (and not on private individuals or entities such as companies), sometimes those obligations will require *positive* action on the part of the state to protect an individual's rights from violation by other private individuals or bodies.[45]

One way in which to achieve the above objective would be to include a clause in the Incorporation Act which stipulated that domestic courts should construe the ECHR in accordance with the case-law of the European Court of Human Rights and, in the absence of any such case-law, in accordance with

[40] See Case 152/84 *Marshall* v. *Southampton & South West Hampshire Area Health Authority* [1986] ECR 723.

[41] *Supra* n. 15 at 76.

[42] Under the procedure governed by RSC Ord 53. See *R* v. *City Panel on Takeovers and Mergers, ex p. Datafin plc* [1987] QB 815 (CA); cf. *R* v. *Disciplinary Committee of the Jockey Club, ex p. Aga Khan* [1993] 1 WLR 909 (CA).

[43] See, for the responsibility of an employer for the acts of employees in the similar context of racial discrimination under existing legislation, *Jones* v. *Tower Boot Co Ltd* [1997] 2 All ER 406 (CA).

[44] *Supra* n. 15 at 76. It has to be said that this, together with the language of "fundamental law" which is used elsewhere in the paper, gives what is proposed a very different flavour from ordinary Acts of Parliament. It is similar to the status of EC law, under which positive action may be required even by Parliament: see *R* v. *Secretary of State for Employment, ex p. Equal Opportunities Commission* [1995] 1 AC 1.

[45] See, for example, *Young, James and Webster* v. *United Kingdom*, Series A, No. 44 (1982) 4 EHRR 38 in the context of the right to freedom of association in Article 11 of the ECHR; *Plattform "Ärzte für das Leben"* v. *Austria*, Series A, No. 139 (1991) 13 EHRR 204.

that of the European Commission of Human Rights. This would have the more general advantage of ensuring that domestic courts did not fall out of step with the requirements of the ECHR as authoritatively interpreted in Strasbourg. This will be important to minimise the occasions when challenges are made in Strasbourg to acts of the United Kingdom, which will still be possible after incorporation. This provision would be similar to section 3(1) of the European Communities Act 1972, which provides that, in the interpretation of EC law, national courts and tribunals must decide in accordance with relevant principles laid down by, and any decision of, the European Court of Justice and any court attached to it.

To What Extent Should the Incorporation Act be "entrenched"?

The most important provision in an Incorporation Act is likely to be the one that tries to relate the Incorporation Act to other Acts of Parliament. It is possible to have a variety of models of Bills of Rights, some of which will have more appeal than others in the United Kingdom.

It is in theory possible to have a "strong" Bill of Rights such as those in the United States Constitution and in the Constitution of the Federal Republic of Germany. These are, however, relatively unusual even in the democratic world. A strong Bill of Rights has the status of a supreme law, which cannot be amended or repealed except by some special constitutional procedure: in the US Constitution this requires a two-thirds majority in both Houses of Congress and passage by the legislatures of three-quarters of the states.[46] This procedure is deliberately cumbersome and has been successfully used only infrequently and hardly ever in order to reverse a decision of the US Supreme Court. Few people advocate a strong Bill of Rights for the United Kingdom. It would be inconsistent with the important role of Parliament in our system and the difficulty of amendment would give much more power to the courts, which would have to interpret the Incorporation Act, than most people find acceptable in a democracy.

At the other end of the spectrum are what I would call "weak" Bills of Rights. These are capable of amendment or repeal by ordinary legislation. The doctrine of "implied repeal", according to which a later Act of Parliament which is inconsistent with an earlier one impliedly repeals the earlier one in so far as there is an inconsistency, may be held to apply even to a fundamental rights Act.[47]

Sometimes a Bill of Rights includes a requirement that a minister should certify to Parliament that a proposed measure before it complies with the Bill of Rights. This is what is required by the New Zealand Bill of Rights, which

---

[46] Article V of the US Constitution.
[47] See *Ellen Street Estates Ltd* v. *Minister of Health* [1934] 1 KB 590; E C S Wade & A W Bradley, *Constitutional and Administrative Law* 11th edn, (London, Longman, 1993) at 76–7.

was enacted in 1990 and which provides an example which is of interest to the United Kingdom because of the similarities between the two countries in legal and political culture. It is, of course, possible to have a combination of methods, a "belt and braces" approach to effective implementation of human rights, which is to be applauded. In the Report of the Joint Consultative Committee on Constitutional Reform it is proposed that there should be a combination of executive, legislative and judicial vigilance for the protection of human rights. Under the Report's recommendations, ministers would, when introducing Bills into Parliament, be required to explain why any provision is, or appears to be, inconsistent with the ECHR. As the Report points out:

> "This would strengthen Parliamentary scrutiny and aid the courts in interpreting Parliament's intentions in legislating."[48]

Furthermore, the Report recommends that there should be a Joint Select Committee of both Houses of Parliament to monitor the operation of the Incorporation Act, scrutinise pending legislative measures in the light of the ECHR, and advise Parliament about compliance with the United Kingdom's obligations under the international human rights codes to which it is party – measures which go well beyond the ECHR.[49]

In the middle of the spectrum are "intermediate" Bills of Rights. These can be altered by later Act of Parliament but not as easily as if they were an ordinary statute. Often they contain what is known as a "legislative override" clause. This enables Parliament to act in breach of the Bill of Rights but only if it so states in clear language. Sometimes the clause requires that the legislative override should take effect only for a limited period, following which it must be reviewed. The Canadian Charter of Fundamental Rights and Freedoms provides an example of this intermediate kind of Bills of Rights.[50]

I would suggest that the intermediate type is right for this country. This seems to be the intention behind "Bringing Rights Home" which says:

> "The courts would be required to construe all existing (as well as future) legislation, as far as is possible, consistently with the Convention."[51]

This language is very similar to that of the Bill introduced by Lord Lester in early 1997, which was expressly based on the New Zealand model.[52]

But the language could be clearer: if Parliament wishes to protect an Incorporation Act from anything but express repeal, it should say so. If that

---

[48] Para. 19.
[49] Para. 21.
[50] See section 33 of the Charter.
[51] *Supra* n. 15 at 75.
[52] In fact, Lord Lester's Bill was much closer to the Hong Kong Bill of Rights Ordinance 1991. The New Zealand model is remarkable because (in section 4) it makes the Bill of Rights subordinate to *past* as well as future Acts of Parliament and in terms disapplies the doctrine of implied repeal which would otherwise apply.

is not its purpose, it should be.[53] There is already a precedent in UK law which we can rely on in order to achieve this aim. We are already used to a system of supranational law which has supreme status in our legal system: European Community law. It is for the time being the nearest thing we have to a fundamental Constitution. It would be possible for the United Kingdom to withdraw from the European Union so far as this country's courts are concerned, and they would respect Parliament's decision to do so.[54] However, in the absence of such a drastic move, the courts will construe all Acts of Parliament, including those that were enacted after the European Communities Act 1972, in such a way as to take effect "subject to" the requirements of directly effective Community law: those are the magic words of section 2(4) of that Act. Those words have been construed by the House of Lords as requiring that, whenever an Act is passed, whether before or after the coming into force of that provision on 1 January 1973, a section is read into it which says that: "the Act is to be construed and shall take effect without prejudice to directly enforceable Community rights."[55] Since we have twenty-five years of experience of what that wording requires, it would be sensible to use similar language in an Incorporation Act to make the ECHR part of domestic law. Adapting the language of section 2(4), an Incorporation Act could provide that "any enactment passed or to be passed shall be construed and have effect subject to the provisions of this Act." As the paper "Bringing Rights Home" says,[56] the Convention, once incorporated, is likely to have a high degree of permanence. The above formula would make it clear that only express repeal (in full or in part) of the Incorporation Act would suffice to require a later Act to supersede the Incorporation Act. This would be consistent with the courts' approach in relation to European Community law.

The argument that this would bind a future Parliament not to derogate from the Convention in times of emergency is met by the point made later in the paper:[57] an express provision limited in duration and subject to parliamentary scrutiny would permit such action.

I am encouraged in my view by the fact that a lawyer as eminent as Sydney Kentridge QC (who has sat on the South African Constitutional Court) takes a similar view. As he put it in his 1996 Harry Street Lecture:

---

[53] This seems to have been the intention behind Lord Lester's 1997 Incorporation Bill: see Lord Lester of Herne Hill QC, "First Steps Towards a Constitutional Bill of Rights" [1997] EHRLR 124 at 128–9.

[55] This was the view of Lord Steyn in his 1996 Annual Lecture to the Administrative Law Bar Association: "The Weakest and Least Dangerous Department of Government" [1997] PL 84 at 85. It was also the view of Sydney Kentridge QC in his 1996 Harry Street Lecture: "Parliamentary Supremacy and the Judiciary under a Bill of Rights: Some Lessons from the Commonwealth" [1997] PL 96 at 104.

[55] See *R* v. *Secretary of State for Transport, ex p. Factortame Ltd* [1990] 2 AC 85 at 140B–C (Lord Bridge of Harwich).

[56] *Supra* n. 15 at 77.

[57] *Ibid.*

"The real objection to following the New Zealand pattern is that it would negate the real purpose of incorporating the Convention – which is to give British judges the same powers as the judges of the European Court of Human Rights. What would be the point of incorporation if the House of Lords still had to say to a litigant at the end of the day – 'This act of Parliament may be a serious and unjustifiable infringement of your rights under the Convention but we cannot say as much. However, if you go to Strasbourg they might be able to help you there.'"[58]

Moreover, if the same hypothetical litigant had approached the court with a complaint under directly effective EC law, the court would have had no need to desist from action; indeed, it would have been required by EC law to protect the right in question.

What Should be the Remedies for Breach of the ECHR under Domestic Law?

The main remedies that could be provided for are the following:

(1) An application for judicial review: this is the normal procedure for bringing complaints about the legality of action by public bodies. The remedies sought are usually the prerogative orders, such as *certiorari*, which is an order which sets aside a decision, and can include injunctions and damages. The procedure is governed by RSC, Ord.53.

(2) As a defence to criminal or civil proceedings.

(3) Exclusion of evidence in criminal (and perhaps) civil proceedings.

(4) Damages.

(5) Restitution: this is an action for recovering money which has been exacted in circumstances where a person would be unjustly enriched unless they pay money back, for example, if a levy is paid pursuant to a demand which the authorities had no power to make.

It should not be assumed that the only, or even the most common, way in which the Incorporation Act will be used will be in applications for judicial review. Clearly this will be an important procedure in many cases and in some of the high profile ones, where perhaps there is a challenge to a controversial decision made by central government or by Parliament itself. Examples from recent history that would have been dealt with under an incorporated ECHR include the *Brind*[59] and *Smith*[60] cases. However, I suspect that in practice the most frequent use of the Incorporation Act will be as a defence to criminal

---

[58] S Kentridge QC, "Parliamentary Supremacy and the Judiciary under a Bill of Rights: Some Lessons from the Commonwealth" [1997] PL 96 at 103–4. An example is provided by the decision of the Court of Appeal (Criminal Division) in *R* v. *Morrissey* Times Law Reports, 1 May 1997, where Lord Bingham of Cornhill CJ, a supporter of incorporation of the ECHR, held (inevitably under existing law) that a provision in an Act which was in breach of the ECHR had to be applied by national courts. See also B. Emmerson, "The Year's Model: Options for Incorporation" [1997] EHRLR (forthcoming).

[59] *R* v. *Secretary of State for the Home Department, ex p. Brind* [1991] 1 AC 696.

[60] *R* v. *Ministry of Defence, ex p. Smith* [1996] QB 517.

cases.[61] Typical examples would include where demonstrators are charged with obstruction of the highway or criminal damage and rely on the rights to freedom of expression and freedom of assembly.[62]

Issues will also frequently arise as to whether the police have breached the ECHR in obtaining evidence, for example if they have engaged in undercover surveillance which arguably interferes with the right to respect for private life in Article 8 of the ECHR.

One question that will arise which will, on the experience of other countries, be controversial is the extent to which breach of the Incorporation Act should lead to the evidence which has been obtained being excluded from use in a criminal trial. This is sometimes called the 'exclusionary rule.'[63] Traditionally English law has not regarded the fact that evidence was obtained illegally as a ground for the exclusion of evidence. This was recently affirmed by the House of Lords in the context of an arguable breach of Article 8 of the ECHR where the police had used a bugging device which was attached to the outside wall of a house and so required some criminal damage to property.[64] However, as the House of Lords also said in the same case, a breach of such rights may lead to the exclusion of evidence if it results in unfairness in the proceedings themselves. This gives one a clue as to the proper use of the exclusionary rule under an Incorporation Act. It should be made clear, either by reference to section 78 of the Police and Criminal Evidence Act 1984[65] or in a similar new provision, that breach of the Incorporation Act will give a trial judge the discretion to exclude evidence if fairness so requires. This would also accord with the case-law of the Strasbourg organs on the relationship between substantive rights such as the right to respect for private life and the right to a fair criminal trial in Article 6(2) of the ECHR.[66]

On the question of damages, in my view "Bringing Rights Home" adopts too cautious an approach. The starting point should be that, if someone has suffered quantifiable loss as a result of a breach of a right in the Incorporation Act, they should be compensated for it. This is not only fair to that person (who may have lost his or her livelihood), it also encourages respect for and

---

[61] See S Kentridge QC, "Parliamentary Supremacy and the Judiciary under a Bill of Rights: Some Lessons from the Commonwealth" [1997] PL 96 at 107–8.[62] See further *infra* Chapter 4.

[63] See for examples in the US case-law *Weeks* v. *United States* 232 US 383 (1914), in which the exclusionary rule was applied to federal enforcement officers; *Mapp* v. *Ohio* 367 US 643 (1961), in which the rule was extended to state police officers; and *United States* v. *Leon* 468 US 897 (1984), in which a so-called "good faith" exception to the rule was devised by the US Supreme Court.

[64] *R* v. *Khan (Sultan)* [1996] 3 WLR 162 (HL).

[65] This provides that: "In any proceedings the court may refuse to allow allow evidence on which the prosecution proposes to rely to be given if it appears to the court that, having regard to all the circumstances, including the circumstances in which the evidence was obtained, the admission of the evidence would have such an adverse effect on the fairness of the proceedings that the court ought not to admit it."

[66] *Schenk* v. *Switzerland* Series A, No. 140 (1991) 13 EHRR 242.

compliance with the rights in the ECHR. Other countries, either through statute or at common law, recognise that there should be a right to damages for at least some violations of a Bill of Rights.[67] This could be important where, for example, evidence has been obtained in breach of the ECHR but either is not used in a criminal trial (so no issue of excluding the evidence arises) or the trial judge decides that fairness does not require the evidence to be excluded. It does not follow that a person whose rights have been violated should be left without any remedy: that person may be the innocent party whose house has been bugged in order to obtain evidence against another person. Where the person concerned is himself or herself concerned in criminal activity, there could be appropriate rules to reduce or deny the claim for compensation (see below).

In addition, it should be possible for exemplary damages to be awarded in what the consultation paper calls "very serious and exceptional cases". In other words, the test suggested in the paper is more appropriate to the question of exemplary damages and is similar to the situations envisaged in existing English case-law on such damages for torts, and not to the question of *compensatory* damages.[68] The Incorporation Act should make clear that courts will have jurisdiction to grant exemplary damages in suitable cases. In the absence of such an express provision, existing case-law suggests that the courts would not have that jurisdiction on the ground that the "tort" concerned did not exist at the time of the House of Lords decision in *Rookes* v. *Barnard*.[69]

This would also have the virtue of being consistent with the general approach to the protection of human rights in EC law. For example, in cases of sex discrimination contrary to the Equal Treatment Directive, compensation has to be paid for all loss actually incurred.[70] It would also avoid potential anomalies where different "fundamental" rights would be actionable in damages depending on their source. For example, some breaches of the Incorporation Act would involve trespass to land, personal property or to the person (for example, false imprisonment) and so would be actionable at common law anyway. Others would not: for example, breach of the right to respect for private life or freedom of assembly, since the common law has not to date given these rights positive protection.[71] Furthermore, suppose that the

---

[67] Zander, *supra* n. 2 at 151–2 and the footnotes there; *Simpson* v. *Attorney-General* (Baigent's case) [1994] 3 NZLR 667; cf. Lord Lester of Herne Hill QC, *supra* n. 52 at 130.

[68] *Rookes* v. *Barnard* [1964] AC 1129.

[69] *Ibid*. See further *AB* v. *South West Water Services* [1993] QB 507 (CA); *Deane* v. *Ealing LBC* [1993] ICR 329 (EAT, a case on racial discrimination); and *Ministry of Defence* v. *Meredith* [1995] IRLR 539 (EAT, a case on sex discrimination).

[70] Case C–271/91 *Marshall* v. *Southampton and South West Hampshire Area Health Authority (No. 2)* [1993] ECR I–4367.

[71] On the right to privacy, see *infra* Chapter 5; on the absence of a common law right to freedom of assembly, see *DPP* v. *Jones* [1997] 2 All ER 119 and *supra* Chapter 1.

Incorporation Act includes a freestanding right to equality like the one contained in Article 26 of the International Covenant. Discrimination would then be prohibited on various grounds that are not currently outlawed (at least in English law), such as sexual orientation or religious opinion.[72] Yet, in the absence of a remedy in damages, people who were discriminated against on those grounds would be at a disadvantage compared to those who are able to bring claims under existing race relations and sex discrimination legislation, which expressly provides for claims in damages. Finally, it should be made clear that a claim for damages may include a claim for injury to feelings, as in the case of the race relations and sex discrimination legislation.[73]

In so far as it may be of concern that unmeritorious plaintiffs (such as those who were engaged in criminal activities or planning terrorist acts) might be awarded compensation, this could be avoided by providing that the court could reduce or deny damages on defined grounds such as illegality or contributory fault. Similar tests are already used in tort law and in the unfair dismissal legislation.[74]

A cautious approach was taken by the latest attempt by Lord Lester of Herne Hill QC to get a human rights Bill passed by Parliament in early 1997. No doubt for pragmatic reasons his Bill on this occasion omitted the provision for damages to be awarded for breach of statutory duty contained in his earlier Bill in 1995. In a speech in the House of Lords when the 1997 Bill was before that House, Lord Woolf gave his weighty support to incorporation of the ECHR. However, in the course of that speech Lord Woolf made a point of principle against the award of damages for breach of the ECHR, which deserves serious consideration.[75] He said:

> "This is important because it is the tradition in this country, so far as the control of public bodies is concerned, that the courts are not primarily concerned with the enforcement of personal rights but the enforcement of public duties. That is why in the ordinary way one does not get damages on an application for judicial review.
>
> I attach great importance to the approach that we have to the enforcement of public duties rather than private rights. I regard that as being a healthy state of affairs. I do not myself want to move the emphasis in that area from public duty to private rights . . . I regard it as very important that public bodies should do what Parliament required them to do, but I consider it unhealthy and unattractive that that should result in damages being awarded for alleged breaches of private rights. It is much better that we should continue with our discretionary use of our prerogative remedies when in the majority of situations there is no need for any form of compensation, although I recognise that if this Bill becomes law there will be a minority of situations where compensation will be appropriate."

[72] See further B Hepple *et al.*, *Improving Equality Law: The Options* (London, Justice, 1997). I must declare an interest: I was a member of the working party that wrote this report.

[73] See section 57(4) of the Race Relations Act 1976 and section 66(4) of the Sex Discrimination Act 1975.

[74] See *Clerk and Lindsell on Torts* 17th edn (London, Sweet & Maxwell) ch. 3; section 123 of the Employment Rights Act 1996.

[75] *Hansard* HL Deb 5 February 1997, col 1736.

With great respect to Lord Woolf, whose support for incorporation (along with that of the present Lord Chief Justice and his late predecessor) has been of invaluable importance, I take a different view as to the nature of a Bill of Rights. Its aim is not primarily to control the powers of public bodies, although that is one of its effects. Its primary purpose is to give every one of us a set of rights which surround us with a zone of protection into which the state may not intrude except for good reason and after due process, rights which touch on fundamental aspects of the human personality such as physical security and matters of conscience.[76] It is right, in principle, that when those rights are violated and someone suffers a loss as a result, they should receive compensation for it.

If restitution is to be available as a remedy, there is a practical problem which should be resolved at the same time as incorporation. At present, the rules which govern an application for judicial review in RSC Ord. 53 do not permit an action for restitution to be joined in such an application: a claim for damages can be made in such an application.[77] The Law Commission has recommended that a claim for restitution should be capable of being made in such proceedings.[78] At present two sets of proceedings have to be brought: this is wasteful of costs and time.

Should There Be a Human Rights Commission?

For some time it has been suggested that there should be a Human Rights Commission, along the lines of the Commission for Racial Equality and the Equal Opportunities Commission, with responsibility for the promotion and protection of human rights in the United Kingdom.[79] It seems as if there will be a Human Rights Commission established as part of the package of measures introduced by an Incorporation Act.[80] This is to be welcomed. I address here some of the questions that have been raised as to the creation and role of such a commission, in particular by the IPPR's consultation paper (published in December 1996).

---

[76] For a similar idea, see the concept of rights as "an invisible fence over which the state will not be allowed to trespass" used by Wilson J in the Canadian case of *Morgentaler* v. *The Queen* [1988] 1 SCR 30 at 164.

[77] RSC, Ord. 53, r. 7.

[78] Law Com No. 226, *Judicial Review and Statutory Appeals* (1994) para. 8.5.

[79] See Lord Irvine of Lairg QC, "The Legal System and Law Reform Under Labour" in D Bean (ed.), *Law Reform for All* (London, Blackstone, 1996) ch. 1; Zander, *supra* n. 2 at 156–60; S Spencer & I Bynoe, "A Human Rights Commission for the UK – Some Options" [1997] EHRLR 152; and the same authors' consultation paper with the same title for the IPPR, published in December 1996.

[80] See the Report of the Joint Consultative Committee on Constitutional Reform (March 1997) para. 22, which says: "A Human Rights Commission or Commissioner, or similar public body, would provide advice and assistance to those seeking the protection of the rights enshrined in the Convention, and be itself able to secure effective compliance with the ECHR, whether by judicial review or by representative proceedings on behalf of a number of people."

(1) What is the most important of the Commission's objectives? Enforcement. Advice and education are plainly important as well but ultimately the effectiveness of the Commission (and any Human Rights Act which it is charged with implementing) will be judged by whether it takes targeted enforcement action. This is why the Equal Opportunities Commission (EOC) in particular has earned respect.

(2) Should the existing commissions such as the EOC be merged with the new Commission? No. The existing Commissions and other bodies such as the Office of the Data Protection Registrar have limited remits and should be left to get on with them. Any overlap in the work of the new Commission and the existing bodies is limited and, in practice, it is likely that the bodies concerned would work together to avoid duplication of effort. The task of merging the existing bodies would distract energy because they are likely to resist this; pragmatically, therefore, it would be better to circumvent the likely opposition to merger by creating a separate Human Rights Commission. Finally, the work of the existing Commissions tends to concern *private* entities or public bodies exercising private functions, for example as employers: the Commissions issue codes of practice for equal opportunities at the workplace. The Human Rights Commission (if the ECHR is incorporated along the lines suggested above) is likely to be concerned primarily with *public* bodies exercising *public* functions.

(3) Should the Commission be able to bring legal proceedings? Yes. One of the most important cases decided by the courts in recent years is the EOC's application for judicial review of the United Kingdom's failure to give part-time workers unfair dismissal rights.[81] No doubt in most cases, like the EOC, the Human Rights Commission would target test cases by supporting individual applicants or by intervening in existing proceedings (I deal with public interest intervention in more detail in Chapter 7). However, for the avoidance of doubt, the Commission should expressly be given standing to bring court proceedings in its own name as well.

(4) Should there be one Commission for the whole of the United Kingdom or separate ones for Northern Ireland and Scotland? Separate ones. Apart from the reasons set out in the IPPR paper, this is because Scotland is likely to have its own Parliament and Northern Ireland may have an Assembly again. Separate commissions in those jurisdictions could advise those devolved bodies.

(5) Should there be one Commissioner or a body of Commissioners? A body of Commissioners. This would allow for diverse membership. Where there is a single person who performs certain functions, such as

---

[81] *R* v. *Secretary of State for Employment, ex p. Equal Opportunities Commission* [1995] 1AC 1.

the Director-General of Fair Trading, appointees tend to be lawyers. The Chairperson of the Human Rights Commission should not necessarily be a lawyer. A high-profile Chairperson of the Commission, with obvious independence and integrity, should be appointed.

(6) Should the Commission be able to receive private funding? Yes, but only from charitable foundations such as those that already support civil liberties work. If (say) newspaper proprietors could make large donations to the Commission, its perceived independence might be undermined and the fear that human rights such as freedom of speech tend in practice to be the preserve of the rich and powerful would be given some credibility.

(7) Is a parliamentary committee enough to fulfil the Commission's functions? No. Human rights are too important to be left to any branch of the state itself. If Parliament scrutinised its own legislation more carefully to avoid breaches of human rights principles, that would be welcome. However, as I have outlined above, most cases (historically at least) under the ECHR have tended to involve not legislation but administrative practices or rules of the common law. The Commission could keep these under scrutiny.

In my view, there is a need for an expert Commission, especially in the early years after incorporation, otherwise the attempt to graft a human rights culture onto existing legal and political arrangements could go sadly wrong.

Should There Be a Separate Constitutional Court?

It should be made clear in an Incorporation Act that reliance on the ECHR would be possible in any court, tribunal or administrative body. For example, it would be available as a defence to criminal prosecution or to enforcement action in the planning context, even though it might in theory have been possible to challenge the decision by initiating proceedings. I agree with the paper "Bringing Rights Home" that there should not be a separate constitutional court. In a legal system which is already complicated by the division between private law and public law procedures and where points of EC law often have to be referred to Luxembourg, introducing a new court would create new demarcation disputes about jurisdiction and references to it.

"Bringing Rights Home" suggests that:

> "Where an unusually difficult or controversial human rights issue arises in a lower court or tribunal, we favour a fast-track route to the higher courts for a prompt decision."[82]

I agree that this would be sensible. There is a precedent for "leap-frog" appeals in cases that are heard by the House of Lords without going through

---

[82] Supra n. 15 at 74.

the Court of Appeal. The procedure would have to be devised with care, how-ever. What most judges value, as many advocates will have found in practice, is the opportunity to consider the judgments of lower courts that have grap-pled with the points of law before them. If the leap-frog procedure misses out too many stages in the judicial hierarchy, the House of Lords may not have the benefit of well-argued judgments below: an example might be if a case went straight from the lay magistrates' court to the House of Lords.

As the paper "Bringing Rights Home" hints may be done (although its authors are not convinced of the merits of the proposal), it would be a good idea to co-opt non-lawyers to sit on important appeals in the House of Lords which concern human rights. The concept of human rights is political and philosophical in origin: lawyers are not the only (or necessarily the best) peo-ple to debate such issues. There is also the practical point that, in controver-sial cases, the legitimacy of the court is likely to be enhanced if it includes people from outside the law. The sort of people who would be suitable are those who have obvious experience of human rights but are not qualified lawyers, such as Baroness Warnock or Lord Runciman. Their experience would be invaluable in cases which raise issues such as the right to life in sen-sitive medical cases and the right to silence in criminal procedure. It is not unprecedented for non-lawyers to sit on a court that has to decide points of law: in the Employment Appeal Tribunal the lay members can even outvote the judge who presides over a case. What I have in mind for the House of Lords is not that the lay members would be in a majority or even that there should be more than one in any given case but that, in suitable cases, they could sit by invitation of the Lord Chancellor.

CONCLUSION

I am encouraged that at long last it seems as if this country will bring human rights home. But if the passage is to be a smooth one, it would be as well to plan for the difficult and technical questions that lie in the way. I hope that the debate will continue but that it will focus on how to make incorporation effective: not on whether we should have incorporation but how best to achieve it.

3

Of Myth and Reality: The Judges as Guardians of Human Rights[1]

It may seem perverse but a century which has justifiably been called the "Age of Extremes",[2] a century that has seen (so far as we know) unprecedented barbarism, can also (without sarcasm) be regarded as the "Age of Rights". Since World War II, in particular, the age-old problem of whether there are human rights and where they come from – whether from pure reason, natural law, divine origin or universal custom – has been largely avoided, if not resolved, by the social fact that the international community has come to accept a set of principles as being of global application. In a process beginning with President Franklin Roosevelt's Four Freedoms, through the Universal Declaration of Human Rights to the two International Covenants which implemented the Declaration as a matter of legal obligation, the world has come to adopt an international Bill of Rights. Regional systems for the protection of human rights have also been established in Europe, the Americas and in Africa. As Professor Bobbio puts it in his book, *The Age of Rights*:

"The fundamental problem concerning human rights today is not so much how to justify them, but how to protect them. This problem is political, not philosophical."[3]

I would add that the problem is also a *legal* one. With that end in mind, the theme which I hope links this and other essays is "making human rights effective". In Chapter 6 I look at an example of the way in which some human rights have a superior, indeed supreme, status in domestic law as a result of their reception through European Community ("EC") law; I have taken freedom of movement as an example, not only because it is in itself a human right but also because I hope to show that imaginative arguments can be made on the basis of it to give indirect effect to such human rights as freedom of expression. My last chapter looks at procedural issues, such as the standing of groups to bring applications for judicial review and third-party intervention in proceedings that have been begun by other people; although such topics have more general application to public law and indeed private law, I will suggest that one of the ways in which to make human rights more effective is

---

[1] This essay is based on a seminar given at Queen Mary and Westfield College, London on 2 October 1996, chaired by Lord Steyn.

[2] E. Hobsbawm, *The Age of Extremes: The Short Twentieth Century* (London, Abacus, 1994).

[3] N Bobbio, *The Age of Rights* (tr. Allan Cameron, Oxford, Polity Press, 1996) at 10.

to ensure that public interest litigation is encouraged, not hampered, by our legal system.

In this chapter I would like to look at three myths which relate to the proper role of judges in the protection of human rights in a democratic society such as ours:

(1) The myth that human rights are already adequately protected by English administrative law, in particular by the doctrine of *Wednesbury* unreasonableness.
(2) The myth of judicial supremacism, that there is something undemocratic about judicial enforcement of human rights.
(3) The myth of negative rights, that the only human rights are civil and political rights and that these are negative in character.

THE MYTH OF ADEQUATE PROTECTION BY *WEDNESBURY* UNREASONABLENESS

In Chapter 1 I have already tried to outline the position, as I understand it, which the English courts have now reached in affording protection to human rights.[4] However, I should set out again the statement of principle formulated by David Pannick QC and endorsed by the Court of Appeal in *R* v. *Ministry of Defence, ex p. Smith*:

> "The court may not interfere with the exercise of administrative discretion on *substantive grounds* save where the court is satisfied that the decision is unreasonable in the sense that it is beyond the range of responses open to a reasonable decision-maker. But in judging whether the decision-maker has exceeded this margin of appreciation the human rights context is important. The more substantial the interference with human rights, the more the court will require by way of justification before it is satisfied that the decision is reasonable in the sense outlined above."[5] (*emphasis added*)

That statement of the relevant principle leads me to my first myth: the myth that adequate protection is given to human rights through the doctrine of *Wednesbury* unreasonableness or irrationality. This myth received some judicial support from the European Court of Human Rights in *Vilvarajah* v. *United Kingdom*.[6] The UK Government submitted to the Court in that case that Article 13 of the Convention, which required the Contracting States to provide an "effective remedy" for an alleged breach of Article 3 of the Convention (which prohibits torture and inhuman and degrading treatment or punishment), was satisfied by the availability in English administrative law of the ground of review known as *Wednesbury* unreasonableness, and that this ground entitled the reviewing court to examine the merits of the

[4] Chapter 1 *supra*.
[5] [1996] QB 517 at 554 E–F.
[6] Series A, No. 215, (1992) 14 EHRR 248.

case.[7] The Court of Human Rights accepted this submission, at least in relation to the case before it.[8] The importance of this judgment was noted (unfortunately without more) by the Court of Appeal in *Smith*[9] and to greater purpose by Sedley J in R v. *Secretary of State for the Home Department, ex p. McQuillan.*[10]

It is sometimes suggested that the doctrine of *Wednesbury* unreasonableness is really just the same as the doctrine of proportionality, which is now familiar to English lawyers at least when they come into contact with EC law. Homely metaphors which strike a chord with the English way of doing things are used, such as "one should not use a sledgehammer to crack a nut", the implication being that, if one did, one would obviously be acting in a way which was so unreasonable that no reasonable person could contemplate doing it. I would suggest that there is in fact a fundamental difference between the concept of irrationality and the concept of proportionality and that only a doctrine of proportionality can give proper protection to human rights. Some decisions will be so far in breach of the doctrine of proportionality as to be irrational in the English law sense – but not all.

The distinction between the two doctrines can be illustrated by a case which has nothing to do with human rights but everything to do with fundamental rights: R v. *Chief Constable of Sussex, ex p. International Trader's Ferry Ltd.*[11] That case arose out of demonstrations that were taking place at ports and airports around the country to protest about the export of live animals. In Sussex, the Chief Constable decided to deploy only a limited level of resources to the policing of those demonstrations. Sometimes this would mean that the exporters would have to be turned back in the interests of safety. The applicants, who were exporters of live animals, complained both that the decision was *Wednesbury* unreasonable and that it was contrary to Article 34 of the EC Treaty, which prohibits "quantitative restrictions on exports, and all measures having equivalent effect" as between Member States of the European Union. This, with Article 30, which deals with restrictions on imports, contains one of the fundamental freedoms of the Community legal order: free movement of goods. The Divisional Court held, first, that the Chief Constable's decision was lawful under domestic law because it could not be characterised as irrational, especially as it involved difficult choices as to the allocation of resources.[12] However, the Court went on to quash the decision

---

[7] Series A, No. 215, (1992) 14 EHRR 248 at para. 120 of the Court's judgment.

[8] *Ibid*, at para. 124 of the Court's judgment. Cf. the judgment of the Court in *Chahal* v. *United Kingdom* (Judgment of 15 November 1996) at paras 147–55, where it found a violation of Article 13 because the complaint under Article 3 could not be considered on its merits by a court or similarly effective body in the context of national security.

[9] [1996] QB 517 at 556 (Bingham MR); cf. Simon Brown LJ in the Divisional Court: [1996] QB 517 at 540; and R v. *Secretary of State for the Environment, ex p. NALGO* (1993) 5 Admin LR 785.

[10] [1995] 4 All ER 400 at 422f.

[11] [1996] QB 197 (DC); cf. [1997] 2 All ER 65 (CA).

[12] 211G–H.

because it failed the test of proportionality under Article 36, which permits a *prima facie* breach of Article 34 to be justified by reference to public policy. The Court held that the Chief Constable had got nowhere near to proving that the resources available to police violent demonstrations were inadequate because, for example, he could have asked for assistance from the Home Office through the police authority.[13] So, we have a vivid example of a case where, on the same facts and on the same evidence as to objective justification, the same Court was able to reach totally opposite conclusions because of the difference in doctrine available to it under two legal systems.

The decision of the Divisional Court has now been reversed by the Court of Appeal.[14] The reason for this was that, on new evidence which was (exceptionally) admitted by the Court of Appeal, it was clear to the Court that, even applying the test of proportionality, the Chief Constable could rely on Article 36 to justify his behaviour. It was plain on the evidence that, even if he had made a formal request to the Home Office for extra funds to police the demonstrations, such funds would not have been forthcoming. In *obiter dicta* Kennedy LJ indicated that it might have been possible for the applicants to complain about the stance of the Home Office, without suggesting that such a complaint would have been successful, but that what they could not do was to raise that complaint in proceedings against the Chief Constable. So much for the actual result of that case. The case remains of interest in the human rights context for several reasons. First, Kennedy LJ acknowledged that, in the light of the House of Lords decision in *Brind*,[15] proportionality was not the same as irrationality. Secondly, however, he said that in given cases the two concepts may overlap so much that there is no light between them; in so stating, Kennedy LJ expressly drew assistance from the extra-judicial remarks of Lord Hoffmann in a lecture given in November 1996.[16] Thirdly, Kennedy LJ adopted a passage in the latest edition of de Smith,[17] which suggests that, while the doctrine of proportionality will allow a certain "margin of appreciation" to the decision-maker, who must form the primary judgment on the question, this is so only outside the field of human rights.[18]

---

[13] At 215D–216B.

[14] [1997] 2 All ER 65.

[15] *R v. Secretary of State for the Home Department, ex p. Brind* [1991] 1 AC 696.

[16] Lord Hoffmann, "A Sense of Proportion" (unpublished lecture, 14 November 1996), referred to in *R v. Chief Constable of Sussex, ex p. ITF Ltd* [1997] 2 All ER 65 at 80h.

[17] S A de Smith, Lord Woolf and J Jowell, *Judicial Review of Administrative Action* 5th edn (London, Sweet & Maxwell,1995) at 605.

[18] In the 1996 Annual Lecture to the Administrative Law Bar Association, Lord Steyn also accepted that there is a difference between the two concepts of *Wednesbury* unreasonableness and proportionality. He went on to say (judiciously) that, although a powerful case had been made for recognition of the principle of proportionality in aid of the protection of fundamental human rights, he would not express a concluded view since the issue would have to be considered sooner or later by the House of Lords: see "The Weakest and Least Dangerous Department of Government" [1997] PL 84 at 94.

As will become apparent later in this essay, I am not calling for a "strict" level of scrutiny by judges in any and all cases where the doctrine of proportionality is used. Nor would I want judges to "second guess" the elected branches of government in sensitive areas such as public finance. On the contrary, I support a flexible approach to the doctrine of proportionality, which (as I suggest in Chapter 4) should involve a structured and weighted exercise which is duly alive to both the fundamental right at stake and to the countervailing interests. What I do suggest, however, is that in the context of human rights, in contrast to commercial rights, a stricter degree of scrutiny is required than the English doctrine of *Wednesbury* unreasonableness permits.

Indeed, in *Smith* both the Divisional Court and the Court of Appeal directly held that, in the context of human rights, *Wednesbury* unreasonableness is different from proportionality.[19] They held that, even in that context, the court is unable to lower the threshold of irrationality. At best it is entitled to form a secondary judgment, to assess whether any primary decision-maker could reasonably form the view that the breach of fundamental rights was justified.[20] Whatever the merits or logical sustainability of *Wednesbury* unreasonableness may be in public law generally, it is a wholly inadequate method of protecting human rights, at least as presently used.

Something like proportionality is used as a technique of adjudication in every jurisdiction with which I at least have any acquaintance. In the United States, even apparently absolute rights such as freedom of speech[21] can be abridged – but only if the restriction is narrowly tailored to serve a compelling state interest. In the Canadian Charter of Fundamental Rights and Freedoms, section 1 provides that the rights set out in it are subject only to "such reasonable limits prescribed by law as can be demonstrably justified in a free and democratic society". In many of the provisions of the European Convention,[22] a right may be interfered with only if the interference is prescribed by law, and is necessary in a democratic society to meet one or more of a set of listed governmental aims. The concept of necessity requires both that the interference must meet a "pressing social need" and that the means chosen must be proportionate to the end in view.

It is true that the Strasbourg institutions will afford Contracting States a "margin of appreciation" in deciding whether a measure is proportionate, for example. However, the margin of appreciation is not always wide. For exam-

---

[19] The judgment of Simon Brown LJ in the Divisional Court puts this most clearly: see *supra* n. 10 at 540F.

[20] See also the illuminating commentary on *Smith* by Sydney Kentridge QC in his 1996 Harry Street Lecture: "Parliamentary Supremacy and the Judiciary under a Bill of Rights: Some Lessons from the Commonwealth" [1997] PL 96 at 98–9.

[21] The First Amendment to the US Constitution provides that: "Congress shall make no law . . . abridging the freedom of speech . . ."

[22] For example, Article 8(2), which permits interference with the right to respect for a person's private and family life, home and correspondence if it is prescribed by law and is necessary in a democratic society for the prevention of crime etc.

ple, in the context of freedom of expression, it has often been virtually non-existent;[23] in the context of Article 8 and homosexuality, it was also very narrow.[24] In *NALGO*,[25] Neill LJ expressly drew the distinction between the European concept of a margin of appreciation and the English doctrine of *Wednesbury* unreasonableness. In my view, he was right to do so. Furthermore, the concept of a margin of appreciation was originally devised in the context of a *supranational* system of law, where it is understandable that a court with many nationalities represented on it and which is far removed from the conditions in a given Contracting State may feel that certain questions are best left primarily to *national* authorities (*including* courts).[26] It does not follow from this that the judiciary *within* a Contracting State should automatically defer to the judgment of the executive: whether they should do so will depend on the subject-matter, a topic to which I return later.

As I have mentioned, EC law contains a powerful principle of proportionality which our courts are required to apply when what is at stake is a right protected by Community law. In EC law too, the European Court of Justice adopts a flexible approach to the application of the doctrine of proportionality: it does not always entail a substitution of the judgment of the Court for that of the Community institutions or national authorities whose decision is under challenge. However, the more important a right is in the Community legal order, the more intense the scrutiny adopted by the Court.[27] Even in the case of someone with a terrorist past, the courts will not necessarily defer to the judgment of the authorities concerned.[28]

In my view, the test of proportionality provides the link between declaring rights as aspirations and making them effective in reality. To leave the question of justification to the primary decision-maker is (if I may inelegantly mix two metaphors) to leave the poacher to be judge in his own cause – subject only to asking whether he has gone mad. The most tyrannical regime can with cold rationality violate the rights of those for whom it cares nothing and whom it may despise. A rational restriction is not the same thing as one that is necessary, still less so in a *democratic* society. The legal doctrine of proportionality or necessity is equivalent to the political doctrine that fundamental rights are special because they are like "trump cards" but they are not necessarily absolute: to change the metaphor again, they are surrounded by a high wall of protection, which cannot be breached merely because it would

---

[23] See *Sunday Times* v. *United Kingdom* Series A, No. 30 (1979–80) 2 EHRR 245.

[24] See *Dudgeon* v. *United Kingdom* Series A, No. 45 (1981) 3 EHRR 40.

[25] *R* v. *Secretary of State for the Environment, ex p. NALGO* (1993) 5 Admin LR 785 (CA).

[26] See also R Ryssdall, "The Coming of Age of the European Convention on Human Rights" [1996] EHRLR 18 at 27, discussed *supra* in Chapter 2 at 21–22.

[27] See G de Búrca, "The Principle of Proportionality and its Application in EC Law" [1993] YBEL 105 at 146.

[28] See e.g. *Proll (Astrid) (alias Puttick, Anna)* v. *Entry Clearance Officer, Dusseldorf* [1988] 2 CMLR 387 (IAT).

be desirable or useful that it should be, but the wall is not insurmountable, for example to prevent a public catastrophe.[29]

What then should be done? The answer lies in further development of the common law, so as to permit a court to exercise its own judgment as to the objective justification for an infringement of fundamental human rights (which is unlikely to happen, since the House of Lords refused leave to appeal in *Smith*) and/or in a Bill of Rights to be enacted by Parliament. I am encouraged that the latter is now the declared position not only of the Labour and Liberal Democrat Parties[30] but of senior judges such as Lord Bingham CJ. Whether a Bill of Rights should be entrenched so as to be capable of amendment only by some special constitutional procedure or should be amenable to a legislative override (as I would prefer) is an important question which I have tried to address already.[31] It may be said that enactment of any type of Bill of Rights will lead to a transfer of power from the democratic branches of government to the undemocratic one. This takes me to my second myth: the myth of judicial supremacism, that there is something "undemocratic" about judicial enforcement of human rights.

THE MYTH OF JUDICIAL SUPREMACISM

At first sight it may seem obvious that the judicial enforcement of human rights is undemocratic. Judges in the United Kingdom are not elected either directly by the people or indirectly by the people's representatives. There is nothing even like the system for the Senate's "Advice and Consent" which is required by Article II, section 2 of the US Constitution for the appointment by the President of judges to the Supreme Court. Fear of the "judicialisation" of democracy stems from a sincere concern for democracy, a development of only the last seventy years in this country. The right to vote itself is a vital human right: without it, black people were excluded from other rights, not only in South Africa until recently but in many parts of the USA between 1890 and 1965. In the UK the major political struggle of the nineteenth and early twentieth centuries was the campaign to get the vote, for working-class men and for women.

Some also fear that the judges would be dangerous if they were given the power to enforce some fundamental law, since they would be free to make that law up as they go. This fear is not new. It goes back at least to the founders of the American Republic themselves. When President Jefferson was

---

[29] R Dworkin, *Taking Rights Seriously* (London, Duckworth, 1977) at 191; R Dworkin, *A Bill of Rights for Britain* (London, Chatto & Windus, 1990) at 10: "In a culture of liberty, these freedoms cannot be abridged except to prevent a clear and serious danger – a calamity – and even then only so far as is absolutely necessary to prevent it."

[30] See *supra* chapter 2, at 17–18.

[31] See *supra* Chapter 2 on ways of enacting a Bill of Rights.

informed about the Supreme Court's decision in *Marbury* v. *Madison*[32] that the courts had the power of judicial review over the acts of other branches of government, including Acts of Congress, he said:

"The constitution, on this hypothesis, is a mere thing of wax in the hands of the judiciary, which they may twist and shape into any form they please."[33]

Sometimes the argument against judicial enforcement of human rights stems from a philosophical position that is at best uneasy with the concept of fundamental rights at all. There are those who adhere to the "Cole Porter" theory of democracy, that "Anything Goes". For them, there are no rights and there are no wrongs, only what the majority of people decide. I suppose they would say that my view that genocide is wrong is on a par with my preference for chocolate, rather than vanilla, ice cream. I would suggest that they take a look at some of the enduring images of the twentieth century and ask whether they can be true to themselves in maintaining that view. Those images would include pictures of the victims of the Holocaust; children being shot in Soweto in the worst years of the apartheid régime; and the picture of the student in Tiananmen Square in 1989 standing alone in front of a tank – a picture capturing perfectly the strength of the human spirit but also the scale and brutality of the obstructions in the path of the effective realisation of human rights. In case it be said that those are examples of régimes that were profoundly undemocratic (which is itself questionable in the case of the Nazi régime at least in its early years), it is worth recalling that in one of the earliest democracies of the modern era, the USA, the promise of Lincoln's Emancipation Proclamation of 1863 was frustrated for nearly a century by a party that represented the white working class and whose very name is "Democratic" with a capital D.

It is undeniable that many countries which are in the same democratic mould as the United Kingdom have, when the chance arose, given power to judges to enforce charters of fundamental rights. The United States got there first when the Supreme Court decided *Marbury* v. *Madison*[34] – although that may not have been the intention in 1791, when the first ten amendments, collectively known as the Bill of Rights, were adopted, no serious attempt has been made to abrogate the power of judicial review since 1803.[35] Many

[32] 1 Cranch (5 US) 137 (1803).

[33] Quoted in B Schwartz, *A History of the Supreme Court* (New York, Oxford University Press, 1993) at 53. In the same letter, to Judge Roane, Jefferson said: "[The Constitution] has given, according to this opinion, to one of them [the branches of government] alone, the right to prescribe rules for the government of the others; and to that one too which is unelected by, and, independent of, the nation, for experience has already shewn that the impeachment it has provided is not even a scare crow . . ."

[34] 1 Cranch (5 US) 137 (1803).

[35] Whether the framers of the US Constitution intended the courts to have a power of judicial review has been much debated. Evidence from J Madison, A Hamilton and J Jay, *The Federalist Papers* (original 1788) (Harmondsworth, Penguin, 1987), No. 78, at 439, would suggest that it was: "The interpretation of the laws is the proper and peculiar province of the courts. A

countries in the Commonwealth have followed suit, for example India, Canada and to some extent New Zealand. Most of the Member States of the European Union and the Council of Europe have either enacted their own Bill of Rights, or incorporated the European Convention, or both. Most interestingly perhaps, the new democracies of Eastern Europe and South Africa have chosen some variant of this model: no country, so far as I am aware, has in modern times chosen to write a Constitution based on that of the United Kingdom, in particular to create an unlimited legislature.

Even the United Kingdom has acceded to an international treaty, the European Convention, which in its time at least was unique in that it created a judicial system for the enforcement of the rights set out in it. Not only are the organs which sit in Strasbourg recognisably courts (even though one of them is called a "Commission"); the United Kingdom has also accepted the right of individual petition to the Commission, a procedure that approximates most closely to the traditional legal system, of individual rights which are justiciable before an independent adjudicator.

How are these developments to be reconciled with democracy? To answer this question, it is worth reminding ourselves why democracy is a valued institution of modern societies. It is not just the pragmatic consideration that, as Churchill put it, democracy is the worst form of government except every other. Our commitment to democracy stems from the principle that the only legitimate government is one to which we have consented. But why should our consent matter? It is surely because only through our consent can we be free members of society. In characteristically terse prose, Kant put it this way:

> "Since every restriction of freedom through the arbitrary will of another party is termed *coercion*, it follows that a civil constitution is a relationship between *free* men who are subject to coercive laws, while they retain their freedom within the general union with their fellows."[36]

Constitution is, in fact, and must be regarded by the judges as, a fundamental law . . . Nor does this conclusion by any means suppose a superiority of the judicial to the legislative power. It only supposes that the power of the people is superior to both, and that where the will of the legislature, declared in its statutes, stands in opposition to that of the people, declared in the Constitution, the judges ought to be governed by the latter rather than the former. They ought to regulate their decisions by the fundamental laws rather than by those which are not fundamental."

[36] I. Kant, *Political Writings* (ed. H Reiss) (Cambridge, Cambridge University Press, 1991) at 73. The passage goes on to note that: "Men have different views on the empirical end of happiness and what it consists of, so that as far as happiness is concerned, their will cannot be brought under any common principle nor thus under any external law harmonising with the freedom of everyone.

The civil state, regarded as a purely lawful state, is based on the following *a priori* principles:

1. The *freedom* of every member of society as a *human being*.
2. The *equality* of each with all the others as a *subject*.
3. The *independence* of each member of a commonwealth as a *citizen*.

These principles are not so much laws given by an already established state, as laws by which a state can alone be established in accordance with pure rational principles of external human right." (*original emphasis*).

This same idea of consent animated the first ringing words of the American Declaration of Independence and is to be found in the modern era in Article 21(3) of the Universal Declaration of Human Rights.

For me, there is no dichotomy in principle between democracy and respect for human rights. Both concepts are based on the same understanding of the dignity of human beings:[37] we all have our own identity, a consciousness, a conscience, a history, hopes, feelings and even disappointments, in short this is what makes us moral persons. And we owe every other person endowed with the same qualities the respect that we would expect from them.[38] For anyone, even the majority in a democracy, to abuse their power so as to violate the fundamental rights which make possible a life with dignity is to strike at the heart of the very reason why democracy itself is valuable. It is to deny a person their humanity; it is to make him or her no longer a free and consenting participant in society; it is to commit a fundamental breach of the social contract that binds us together.

Although social contract theories are no longer fashionable, this may be because they were often misunderstood. Kant himself was quite clear that the social contract was not a historical reality but "an *idea* of reason",[39] a cognitive device which helps to explain how we can be free and yet be bound by the rules of a society – it is through our consent to be part of a democratic polity. This is the way to reconcile the apparent contradiction with which Rousseau dramatically began *The Social Contract* when he said: "Man is born free; and everywhere he is in chains."[40]

How is there to be a principled and legitimate role for the judiciary in the implementation of human rights in a democracy? Far be it for a mere practitioner to come up with a comprehensive theory – although we badly need just such a theory and we need scholars in political science and philosophy as well as in the law schools to contribute to that debate. However, I would suggest that a starting-point at least can be found in American scholarship which is based on one of the most famous *obiter* passages in the jurisprudence of the US Supreme Court, in Justice Stone's Opinion in *US v. Carolene Products Co.*[41] One American writer has compared the role of the judge to that of the

---

[37] See Article 1(1) of the Universal Declaration of Human Rights.

[38] This is what Kant called the principle of universalisability or the categorical imperative.

[39] *Supra* n. 34 at 79.

[40] J-J Rousseau, *The Social Contract* (1762, tr. G.D.H. Cole, London, J.M. Dent and Son, 1913) at 1. The passage continues: "How did this change come about? I do not know. What can make it legitimate? That question I think I can answer."

[41] 304 US 144 (1938) at 152–3, n. 4: "It is unnecessary to consider now whether legislation which restricts those political processes which can ordinarily be expected to bring about repeal of undesirable legislation, is to be subjected to more exacting judicial scrutiny under the general prohibitions of the Fourteenth Amendment than are most other types of legislation . . . Nor need we enquire whether similar considerations enter into the review of statutes directed at particular religious . . . or national . . . or religious minorities . . . whether prejudice against discrete and insular minorities may be a special condition, which tends seriously to curtail the operation of those political processes ordinarily to be relied upon to protect minorities, and which may call for a correspondingly more searching judicial inquiry."

referee in a game: "the referee is to intervene only when one team is gaining unfair advantage, not because the 'wrong' team has scored."[42]

There are two underlying themes behind this view: that judicial enforcement of human rights is legitimate because, first, it keeps the democratic process pure, for example it keeps the channels of communication unpolluted, by ensuring that everyone has freedom of speech; and, secondly, it protects what Justice Stone called "discrete and insular minorities" who cannot protect themselves adequately through the franchise.[43] According to the first part of this theory, at least, the apparent contradiction between democracy and judicial enforcement of human rights disappears. The judges are merely supporting democracy, not supplanting it.

The second strand of this theory, however, indicates why it will not do to say that the only legitimate role for judicial enforcement of human rights is the maintenance of democracy. If it is right for the judges to intervene to protect "discrete and insular" minorities – a phrase to which I would today add the epithet "unpopular" – then we cannot avoid the consequence that some substantive outcomes at least will be out of bounds to the majority in society no matter how much they may think them right or desirable. The rights of minorities are not something which the majority can simply trade away because that is how the calculations come out. This is why it is difficult to believe in human rights if you are a utilitarian. Let me digress for a moment to a fictional land invented by Steven Lukes, Utilitaria, founded on the philosophy of Jeremy Bentham, where the purpose of government is the "greatest happiness of the greatest number".[44] In Utilitaria, "what counts is what can be counted. The prized possession of every Utilitarian is a pocket calculator."[45]

---

[42] J Hart Ely, *Democracy and Distrust* (Cambridge, Massachusetts, Harvard University Press, 1980) at 103. He also uses the analogy of an "anti-trust" approach to economic affairs: on that approach interference with the market is justified not to dictate substantive outcomes but to ensure that the market does not systematically malfunction.

[43] As in so many things to do with constitutional law, the problems with which we grapple were anticipated, if not always resolved, by the framers of the US Constitution. In *The Federalist Papers*, No. 78 *supra* n. 36, at 440, it is said that: "The independence of the judges is equally requisite to guard the Constitution and the rights of individuals from the effects of those ill humours which the arts of designing men, or the influence of particular conjunctures, sometimes disseminate among the people themselves, and which, though they speedily give place to better information, and more deliberate reflection, have a tendency, in the meantime, to occasion dangerous innovations in the government, and serious oppressions of the minor party in the community."

[44] S Lukes, "Five Fables about Human Rights" in S Shute & S Hurley (eds), *On Human Rights: The Oxford Amnesty Lectures* (New York, Basic Books, 1993) at 21–2. For further travels through the fictional land of Utilitaria, see S Lukes, *The Curious Enlightenment of Professor Caritat* (London, Verso, 1996) chs 7–14.

[45] See also R Dworkin, *A Bill of Rights for Britain* (London, Chatto & Windus, 1990) at 35–6: "[T]rue democracy is not just *statistical* democracy, in which anything a majority or plurality wants is legitimate for that reason, but *communal* democracy, in which majority decision is legitimate only if it is a majority within a community of equals . . . The rival, pure statistical concept of democracy, according to which democracy is consistent with oppressing minorities, was the concept proclaimed as justification by the Communist tyrannies after the Second World War: they

Where does this leave our judges? It would lead, I suggest, to a different approach first to cases where democracy is at stake. Democracy is not obviously a value recognised by the common law.[46] Yet it is a human right itself.[48] It has implicitly played a part in some English public law cases.[49] This trend could be developed, especially if we have a Bill of Rights. When a public body tries to pollute the democratic process in some way, for example, by using its broad discretionary powers as a landlord to deny certain groups the opportunity to have their say, the court should require that body to show objective justification for its decision, applying a proportionality test.

Secondly, the approach I am advocating would lead the judges to adopt a heightened sense of vigilance in cases where the rights of minorities are affected. In *Smith* the courts were invited to accept that, because it seemed as if Parliament had considered the policy of discharging homosexuals from the armed forces and apparently approved it, there should be an even higher threshold imposed before its rationality could be impugned – what came to be known as the "super-*Wednesbury*" test.[49] This is in effect the test that the courts deploy in cases to do with public finance, in particular where the role of the House of Commons is concerned, since that House has a peculiar constitutional role in money matters. But to have adopted that approach would have been to ignore completely the human rights dimension to the case. A due respect for human rights would, I suggest, lead to the *contrary* conclusion – the view to which the US Supreme Court came in the late 1930s – that, while economic decisions would be left to the other branches of government, provided that they satisfied a "rational basis" standard of judicial scrutiny, where the rights of minorities were at risk of violation by the majority, the courts should apply a "strict scrutiny" standard of review. As we have already seen, the courts rejected that approach in *Smith* and have thus, in my view, left English public law unable to protect human rights adequately.

But the reasons why the judges can legitimately adopt more sensitive antennae where the rights of minorities are concerned are not rooted in principle alone. There are practical virtues as well. The very reason why some people

said democracy meant government in the interests of the masses. The civilised world has recoiled from the totalitarian view, and it would be an appalling irony if Britain now embraced it as a reason for denying minorities constitutional rights." (*original emphasis*)

[46] See, for example, *Bromley LBC* v. *Greater London Council* [1983] 1 AC 768; contrast the attitude of the House of Lords to the importance of a political party's manifesto commitments to that in *Secretary of State for Education and Science* v. *Tameside MBC* [1977] AC 1014. In *R* v. *Somerset County Council, ex p. Fewings* [1995] 1 All ER 513 (Laws J); [1995] 3 All ER 20 (CA) the courts were concerned with apparently pure questions of statutory construction, not whether the fact that a democratically elected local authority could, in a sensitive area of political debate, adopt a moral stance to which the courts should defer.

[47] See Article 21 of the Universal Declaration of Human Rights.

[48] For example, *R* v. *Barnet LBC, ex p. Johnson* (1989) 88 LGR 73 (DC); (1990) 89 LGR 581 (CA).

[49] See especially in the Divisional Court: [1996] QB 517 at 533G–H; 535D–536C. The argument was rejected: 540C–F. The Court of Appeal also rejected it, in briefer terms: 556A–C.

regard judicial protection of human rights as undemocratic is why I consider it to be likely to work. Judges are not susceptible to the same day-to-day pressures that politicians are. Elected politicians rightly look to the immediate effect of their actions on public opinion – and on the likelihood of their getting re-elected next time round. Judges can take a more long-term view, drawing on the enduring values of our society such as equality and fairness. Nor are they necessarily concerned with whether someone has a vote to cast: indeed, it may be that they should intervene precisely because someone (such as the asylum-seeker) does *not* have the vote and so can exercise no political clout through the ballot box.

That is not to say that they should simply make up what the law is: they will be constrained, if not dictated to, by the doctrine of precedent and the methods of common law reasoning with which we are familiar.[50] As Lord Steyn has recently put it:

> ". . . it is important to bear in mind that English judgments are not written in the oracular style of the European Court of Justice: in an English judgment the reasons including policy reasons for the decision are discursively but fully exposed. That facilitates constant public scrutiny of what is done in the name of justice."[51]

It does suggest that they can boldly go where no politician has gone before. The classic instance of this is *Brown* v. *Board of Education*.[52] The politicians, even President Franklin Roosevelt, faced with a conservative majority in his own party that derived its strength in Congress from the American South, did not feel able to challenge racial segregation in education, as the Supreme Court did in that case. The Supreme Court's intervention in the 1950s gave encouragement to the civil rights movement. Liberal politicians, such as President Kennedy, Attorney-General Robert Kennedy and President Johnson then felt able to take up the challenge offered by the courts and promoted the Civil Rights Act of 1964, an Act on which the UK Race Relations and Sex Discrimination Acts are based.[53]

---

[50] See, for example, Dworkin, *supra* n. 27 especially at 110–18 and R Dworkin, *Law's Empire* (London, Fontana Press, 1986) especially chs 6, 7 and 10. The judges are also the "least dangerous" branch of government in the sense used in J Madison, A Hamilton & J Jay, *The Federalist Papers*, (Original 1788) (Harmondsworth: Penguin Books, 1987) No. 78, at 437: ". . . the judiciary, from the nature of its functions, will always be the least dangerous to the political rights of the Constitution . . . The judiciary . . . has no influence over either the sword or the purse; no direction either of the strength or the wealth of society . . . It may truly be said to have neither FORCE nor WILL but merely judgment; and must ultimately depend upon the aid of the executive arm even for the efficacy of its judgments."

See also L Tribe, *God Save This Honorable Court* (New York, Mentor, 1985) at 5: (quoting President Andrew Jackson) "John Marshall has made his decision; now let him enforce it."

[51] Lord Steyn, "The Weakest and Least Dangerous Department of Government" [1997] PL 84 at 85.

[52] 347 US 483 (1954).

[53] For a brilliant history of the litigation strategy and political consequences of *Brown* v. *Board of Education* see R Kluger, *Simple Justice* (New York, Vintage Books, 1977) especially at ix–x and 754.

A more recent example, unfortunately short-lived, is provided by the majority judgment of the Court of Appeal in *R* v. *Secretary of State for Social
Security, ex p. Joint Council for the Welfare of Immigrants*.[54] The Court's
speaking out in favour of the rights of asylum-seekers apparently gave courage
to some politicians to take up their cause. The importance of that case is
something to which I shall return in looking at my third myth, but for the
moment it is further confirmation that Parliament (however imperfect a vehicle for majority opinion it may be) is quite content to do what Simon Brown
LJ said could not be tolerated by any civilised nation: condemn asylum-
seekers to destitution while they pitifully seek to assert legal rights which
Parliament (and international law) have given them.

Finally on the second myth, we cannot ignore the realities of our legal system. The fact is that, like it or not, we in the United Kingdom are members
of the European Union, we do have a fundamental law, EC law and in particular the EC Treaty, and we do have judges, both in national courts and tribunals and at the Court of Justice in Luxembourg, who are called upon to
give effect to the fundamental law in priority to the acts of the other branches
of government, including Acts of Parliament.

What is the consequence of this for human rights? First, as we shall see in
more detail in Chapter 6, some human rights have entered domestic law
through the medium of EC law. But the point I want to stress here is that, so
long as human rights lack a pre-eminent status within our legal system, there
will be a two-tier constitutional system: some rights, those protected by EC law,
which are still predominantly commercial in character, enjoy a favoured status
whereas human rights are vulnerable to a simple majority in Parliament.

THE MYTH OF NEGATIVE RIGHTS

I turn then to the third myth: the myth of negative rights. It is a commonly
held view that the only rights worth protecting, because they alone are fundamental, or perhaps capable of being derived from natural reason, are civil
and political rights. It is also sometimes suggested that civil and political
rights are "negative" rights, and that for that reason they are the only legitimate subjects of judicial protection.[55]

Let me take you to another imaginary land invented by Professor Steven
Lukes: Libertaria, a land founded on the teachings of John Locke[56] where, I
would imagine, "laissez faire" is still a term of praise, not abuse:

---

[54] [1996] 4 All ER 385.

[55] For a powerful defence of the distinction between negative and positive rights, see Sir John
Laws, "The Constitution: Morals and Rights" [1996] PL 622 at 627–35.

[56] Yet Locke said that the end of government is to secure property: what is property if it is
not an *economic* right? See further J Locke, *Second Treatise of Government* (original 1690)
(London, Dent, 1970) ch. VIII.

"No one is tortured in Libertaria. All have the right to vote, the rule of law prevails, there is freedom of expression (in media controlled by the rich) . . . The homeless sleeping under bridges and the unemployed are . . . consoled by the thought that they have the same rights as every other Libertarian."[57]

Nearer to home, Sidney and Beatrice Webb put it this way:

"To some simple minds freedom appears only a negation of slavery. To them any-one is free who is not the chattel of some other person. The shipwrecked mariner on a barren island and destitute vagrant wandering among property-owners pro-tected by an all-powerful police, are 'free men', seeing that they 'call no man mas-ter'. But this sort of freedom is little more than freedom to die. . . . Translated into the terms of daily life, personal freedom means, in fact, the power of the individual to buy sufficient food, shelter and clothing to keep his body in good health, and to gain access to sufficient teaching and books to develop his mind from its infantile state."[58]

It would be wrong to associate this view of the symbiotic relationship between true freedom and social and economic rights only with the socialist movement. In the latter part of the nineteenth century a liberal philosopher called T. H. Green provided the intellectual inspiration for the "New Liberal" government which introduced important social reforms between 1906 and 1914. In defending measures such as compulsory education and workers' pro-tection legislation, Green wrote:

"We shall probably all agree that freedom, rightly understood, is the greatest of blessings; that its attainment is the true end of all our effort as citizens. But when we thus speak of freedom, we should consider carefully what we mean by it. We do not mean merely freedom to do as we like irrespective of what it is that we like. We do not mean a freedom that can be enjoyed by one man or one set of men at the cost of a loss of freedom to others. When we speak of freedom as something to be highly prized, we mean a positive power or capacity of doing or enjoying something worth doing or enjoying, and that, too, something that we do or enjoy in common with others. We mean by it a power which each man exercises through the help or security given him by his fellow-men, and which he in turn helps to secure for them. When we measure the progress of a society by its growth in freedom, we measure

[57] Lukes, "Five Fables about Human Rights" *supra* n. 41 at 32. For further travels in Libertaria, see Lukes, *The Curious Enlightenment of Professor Caritat* (*supra* n. 41), chs 24–9. See also Ely, *supra* n. 39 at 59: "Thus the list of values which the Court and the commentators have tended to enshrine as fundamental is a list with which readers of this book will have little trouble iden-tifying: expression, association, education [why?], academic freedom, the privacy of the home, personal autonomy, even the right not to be locked in a stereotypically female sex role and sup-ported by one's husband. But watch most fundamental-rights theorists start edging toward the door when someone mentions jobs, food or housing: those are important, sure, but they aren't *fundamental*." (*original emphasis*)

[58] S & B Webb, "Inequality of income and inequality of personal freedom" in Lord Desai (ed.), *LSE On Equality* (London, LSE Books, 1995) at 192–3. The passage continues: "Moreover, as we cannot regard as a free man anyone with none but vegetative experiences, freedom involves the command at some time, of at least some money to spend on holidays and travel, on social inter-course and recreation, on placing one's self in a position to enjoy nature and art."

it by the increasing development and exercise *on the whole* of those powers of con-tributing to social good with which we believe the members of the society to be endowed; in short, by the greater power on the part of the citizens as a body to make the most and best of themselves."[59]

Although I am encouraged that UK judges have begun to discover human rights in the common law beyond personal liberty and property in recent years, there must be a danger that as we approach the end of the twentieth century we shall have made progress – but only from 1689 to 1789. If that happened, it would be to ignore the developments of the last two hundred years, in particular the post-war social democratic settlement which occurred in most Western countries and the international Bill of Rights.[60] Indeed, it would be to ignore even Part II of Tom Paine's *The Rights of Man* (first pub-lished in 1792), which advocated an early version of the welfare state.[61]

Another commonly held belief is that the Universal Declaration of Human Rights is to be regarded in the same vein as the European Convention on Human Rights. Both have been called the products of the Enlightenment (and are none the worse for that) and have been said to encapsulate the notion of "possessive individualism".[62] I take a different view. The Universal Declaration is in fact remarkable because, even as the Cold War was starting, it *combined* in the same document the traditional civil and political rights and

---

[59] T H Green, "Liberal Legislation and Freedom of Contract" in T H Green, *Lectures on the Principles of Political Obligation and Other Writings* (P Harris & J Morrow eds) (Cambridge, CUP, 1986) at 199. (*original emphasis*)

[60] See also Bobbio, *supra* n. 3 at 30: "One cannot abstract the problem of human rights from the great problems of our time, which are war and poverty, the absurd contrast between the excess of *power* which created the conditions for a genocidal war and the excess of *impotence* which has condemned the great majority of humanity to hunger. This is the only context in which we can approach the problem of human rights realistically. We must be not so pessimistic that we give up in despair, but neither must we be so optimistic that we become over-confident." (*orig-inal emphasis*)

Also at 18–19: "As we all know, the development of human rights has passed through three stages: the first affirmed the rights to liberty, i.e. all those rights which tend to restrict the power of the state and grants an area of freedom *from* the state to the individual or particular groups. The second stage put forward political rights which perceive freedom not only negatively as non-interference, but positively as autonomy, and therefore have brought about a more wide-ranging and constant involvement by members of a community in the process of political power (or liberties *within* the state). The final stage has proclaimed social rights which express the development of new needs . . . which concern wealth and equality not only on a formal level, and we could call these liberties *through* or *by means of the state*. If someone had told Locke, the champion of the rights to liberty, that all citizens should have the right to participate in politics, or even worse that they had the right to paid employment, he would have called it madness." (*original emphasis*)

[61] (Harmondsworth, Penguin, 1984) at 239–48; see also J Fruchtmann Jr, *Thomas Paine: Apostle of Freedom* (New York, Four Walls Eight Windows, 1994) at 260–2 and 362–3; J Keane, *Tom Paine: A Political Biography* (London, Bloomsbury, 1995) at 302–3. See, for the revolution-ary significance of what Paine was advocating: E P Thompson, *The Making of the English Working Class* (Harmondsworth, Penguin, 1968) at 117–18.

[62] See, for example, Sir Stephen Sedley, "Human Rights: A Twenty First Century Agenda", [1995] PL 386.

social, economic and cultural rights.[63] It seems to have been the product of the social democracies and welfare states of the West rather than the Soviet bloc, since the USSR and its allies in the UN General Assembly abstained when it was adopted; it represented a development of President Roosevelt's "Four Freedoms" (which included freedom from want) and is a tribute to Eleanor Roosevelt's resilience.[64] Even the Council of Europe, which was the sponsor of the European Convention in 1950, did not regard civil and political rights as the only rights worth protecting. It went on to draw up the European Social Charter in 1961, a treaty which is legally binding on the United Kingdom.[65] It is true that no system for individual adjudication was created as it had been under the Convention, but that Convention is virtually unique in international law. The Charter, with a mechanism for reporting to a committee of experts and monitoring by political organs, is more typical of international law than the European Convention: it may not be ideal but it is the best the politicians will let us have.

I would suggest that a rich and proper commitment to human rights in our own time requires that we recognise that social and economic rights are human rights. There is no need to choose between them and civil and political rights. Just as you cannot worship at the temple of liberty if you have nothing to eat, so if you want to protest about people going hungry in a land of plenty you need to have freedom of expression. People rarely demonstrate in the abstract, even in countries that are on the verge of revolution; they protest usually because they have some social or economic goal, whether the call is for "bread and peace" or for the abolition of the Child Support Agency.

But there is another way in which the first and second generation rights (as they are called in international law) are connected. To be effective, even civil and political rights have to be protected – and protection has a price. The right of access to the courts would be meaningless if there were no courts, or if they were not properly financed, or if only a few people could get to them owing to lack of money.[66] In *R v. Lord Chancellor, ex p. Witham*[67] the Divisional Court held that Article 3 of the Supreme Court Fees (Amendment)

[63] The United Kingdom voted for it in the UN General Assembly: the Attlee Government was in power at the time. See G Marston, "The United Kingdom's Part in the Preparation of the European Convention on Human Rights, 1950" (1993) 42 ICLQ 796 at 797–800.

[64] See L Henkin, "The United States and International Human Rights" in American Bar Association, *Justice for a Generation* (St Paul, West Publishing, 1985) 372 at 373–6; D Kearns Goodwin, *No Ordinary Time: Franklin and Eleanor Roosevelt: The Home Front in World War II* (New York, Touchstone Books, 1994) at 201–2; J MacGregor Burns & S Burns, *A People's Charter: The Pursuit of Rights in America* (New York, Alfred A. Knopf, 1991) at 418–24. The Four Freedoms are expressly referred to in the preamble to the Universal Declaration.

[65] A revised version of the European Social Charter was drawn up in 1996 but has not been signed by the United Kingdom. It is to be hoped that the new Labour Government will sign it.

[66] In *Airey v. Ireland*, Series A, No. 32 (1979–80) 2 EHRR 305 the European Court of Human Rights held that Article 6(1) of the Convention will sometimes impose a positive duty on the state to provide legal aid if the complexity and importance of a case render a hearing unfair for a litigant to have to act in person: see para. 26 of the Judgment.

[67] [1997] 2 All ER 779.

Order 1996 was *ultra vires* because it had the effect of denying the constitutional right of access to the courts to people on very low incomes without express authority from Parliament. This is a welcome decision, as I have already suggested,[68] but for the moment I want to concentrate on the following passage in the Judgment of Laws J:

> "Mr Richards [counsel for the Lord Chancellor] submitted that it was for the Lord Chancellor's discretion to decide what litigation should be supported by taxpayers' money and what should not. As regards the expenses of legal representation, I am sure that is right. Payment out of legal aid of lawyers' to conduct litigation is a subsidy by the State which in general is well within the power of the executive, subject to the relevant main legislation, to regulate. But the impost of court fees is, to my mind, subject to wholly different considerations. They are the cost of going to court *at all*, lawyers or no lawyers. They are not at the choice of the litigant, who may by contrast choose how much to spend on his lawyers." *(original emphasis)*[69]

What that passage seems not to recognise is that there may in practice be no distinction between the imposition of fees on the commencement of legal proceedings and the failure by the state to provide legal aid to bring proceedings: each may in substance deny the theoretical right that everyone has to access to the courts. Contrast the approach of the European Court of Human Rights in *Airey* v. *Ireland*[70] where it was held that, in certain circumstances, the failure by the state to provide legal aid in civil proceedings would render the ensuing hearing unfair and so breach Article 6(1) of the European Convention on Human Rights. Even in the United States, which is more of a free market economy than most Western democracies, the Supreme Court's decision in *Gideon* v. *Wainwright*[71] on the right to counsel in criminal cases led to the setting up of public defender offices in most states, with the attendant public expenditure.[72]

The right to life, perhaps the most fundamental of all rights, would surely require of a state more than mere abstention from murdering its citizens. It may require positive action from the state, at least to protect us from killing each other and perhaps to provide some form of health care so that life-threatening illness is treated.[73] Freedom of assembly, according to the European Court of Human Rights, requires a state not merely to abstain from interfering with public gatherings but to afford participants adequate protection from counter-demonstrators.[74] Even privacy, which might be thought to be the quintessential

---

[68] See Chapter 1 *supra*.

[69] At 788 c–d.

[70] *supra* n. 62 at para. 26.

[71] 372 US 335 (1963).

[72] On the jurisprudence of the Strasbourg organs as to positive obligations placed upon Contracting Parties by the European Convention, see D J Harris, M O'Boyle & C Warbrick, *Law of the European Convention on Human Rights* (London, Butterworth, 1995) at 19–22.

[73] See *R* v. *Cambridge Health Authority, ex p. B* [1995] 1 FLR 1055 (Laws J); [1995] 1 WLR 898 (CA, reversing Laws J).

[74] *Plattform "Ärzte für das Leben"* v. *Austria* Series A, No. 139 (1991) 13 EHRR 204, para. 32 of the Court's Judgment.

negative right, postulating a zone of decision-making and action which is reserved to the individual free from state intrusion, requires positive action to be fully "respected": so the European Court of Human Rights has told us in cases about transsexuals and about interception of telephone communications.[75]

What follows for judges? Should they just ignore the fact that the world as a whole regards social and economic rights as human rights? Should they at least wait to see whether Parliament enacts a Bill of Rights including such rights? I would suggest that they need not do so. What matters is how to make effective all the rights which are recognised today to be human rights. I accept that, in many cases, the rights will not be justiciable at the behest of an individual applicant to a court of law. Of course, the will and money to comply with our international obligations in the field of social and economic rights will have to come principally from Parliament and from the executive. A judge is not going to order that someone has the right to a job against the government. But it does not follow that judges are impotent to give effect to such rights when the opportunity does arise, still less that they should be ignored. For to ignore them is to turn the noble promise of the international Bill of Rights into a cruel joke.

Judicial decisions are already beginning to reflect a unified approach to human rights, which acknowledges the symbiotic relationship between social and economic rights and civil and political rights.

The best example is perhaps the Judgment of Simon Brown LJ in the *JCWI* case. This relied on the traditional doctrine that Parliament in conferring a power to make delegated legislation in apparently broad language must be presumed not to authorise legislation that infringes fundamental rights. Traditionally, this would have been confined to interference with personal liberty and property;[76] recently it has been used to protect, for example, what Lord Steyn has called the "constitutional right" of access to the courts;[77] and in *JCWI* it was self-consciously extended to apply to rights to the minimum material goods necessary to make life possible and therefore to make effective the ability of asylum seekers to pursue their claim to asylum in this country. Another encouraging sign about the case was Simon Brown LJ's express reliance on the "law of humanity", a phrase he found in a dictum by Lord Ellenborough CJ in R v. *Inhabitants of Eastbourne*.[78] A discouraging feature of the case was that Parliament reversed the outcome of the Judgment, in spite of efforts of the Upper House to mitigate the harshness of the Asylum and

---

[75] For a recent statement of this principle, in the context of immigration decisions which interfere with the right to respect for family life in Article 8 of the Convention, see *Gül* v. *Switzerland*, Judgment of 19 February 1996, para. 38; and *X, Y, Z* v. *UK*, Judgment of 22 April 1997, para 41 – on the right of transsexuals to respect for family life.

[76] For example, *Attorney-General* v. *Wiltshire United Dairies Ltd* (1921) 19 LGR 534.

[77] R v. *Secretary of State for the Home Department, ex p. Leech* [1994] QB 198 at 210 (Steyn LJ, as he then was).

[78] (1803) 4 East 103: "As to there being no obligation for maintaining the poor foreigners before the statutes ascertaining the different methods of acquiring entitlements, the law of humanity, which is anterior to all positive laws, obliges us to afford them relief, to save from them starving."

Immigration Act 1996. If one believes that Parliament alone will correct abuses of human rights, this sorry episode must be explained.

Another way in which social and economic rights can have an indirect effect on English law is through the well-known doctrine of administrative law that all legally relevant considerations must be taken into account in the exercise of a discretionary power. What could be more relevant than considerations of common humanity: for example, the need that we all have for, and therefore I would say the right to, reasonable shelter and a reasonable standard of health care? Without these the dignity of the human personality of which Kant and others have written is impossible.

But this may have unexpected consequences. For example, the decision of a planning authority to enforce planning controls may be approached differently if it takes into account that a family will be left without a home than if it were enforcing against (say) an unauthorised office use.[79] Likewise, if, in the immigration context, a decision is taken to deport someone whose presence in this country is required (on uncontradicted medical evidence) to enable another person to maintain an adequate standard of health care in the community, the Home Office may be required to take that into account – even though the immigration officer may not have heard of the European Social Charter.[80]

But there are two ways in which the new, unified approach to human rights which I am advocating could affect a judge's perception even of civil and political rights.

First, and perhaps most importantly, if and when we have a Bill of Rights, the court should adopt a stance of relative deference to the judgment of the political organs of the state when they make decisions in the arena of social and economic policy affecting such civil rights as the right to property. One reason for doing this is that Parliament may be trying to implement social and economic rights when, for example, it taxes those who can afford to pay so as to train young people for employment.[81] Just as the theories of Herbert Spencer are not part of the US Constitution, so the merits of redistributive taxation are hardly the province of the judiciary. In this way the dangers of the clash between the US Supreme Court and progressive state and federal governments of the first thirty-five years of this century would be avoided.[82]

Another consequence would be that the court should strive to give a

---

[79] *R* v. *Lincolnshire County Council, ex p. Atkinson and Others*, Times Law Reports, 22 September 1995 (Sedley J); *R* v. *Kerrier DC, ex p. Uzell* (1996) 71 P & CR 566 (Latham J).

[80] In *R* v. *Secretary of State for the Home Department, ex p. Zakrocki* Times Law Reports, 3 April 1996, Carnwath J did not feel it necessary to go into questions relating to international human rights law because he found in favour of the applicant on the traditional English law ground of irrationality, although he acknowledged that the international instruments might be important for other cases.

[81] For an example of the deferential stance of the Strasbourg organs in such cases see *Svenska Managementgruppen AB* v. *Sweden* 45 DR 211 (1985) at 223 where the Commission of Human Rights said: "the Convention leaves it to the Contracting States to determine their political, economic and social policies and Article 1 of Protocol No. 1 to the Convention [which in essence guarantees the right to property] is not intended to protect any specific political view or system."

generous interpretation to civil and political rights so as to ensure that they are real, and not illusory, for everyone on an equal basis. Take the right to freedom of expression. It is well known that those who have the means to shout the loudest can have their say and silence others. This may lead the judge who is interested in making rights effective for everyone to take an expansive view of "speech", to include non-violent direct action, what in America is called "symbolic speech". This would protect the rights of demonstrators, not just those of media moguls. Let me illustrate this with some examples from the American case law: in *Brown* v. *Louisiana*,[83] the Supreme Court held that a silent vigil staged by black students in a library was an act of "speech". As Justice Marshall later put it in *Clark* v. *Community for Creative Non-Violence*: "for Negroes to stand or sit in a 'whites only' library in Louisiana in 1965 was powerfully expressive; in that particular context, those acts became 'monuments of protest' against segregation".[84] *Clark* itself concerned a "sleep in" in Lafayette Park, just outside the White House, to protest about homelessness. The Court decided against the demonstrators because it upheld a rule against sleeping in a national park outside a designated campsite as a reasonable "time, place and manner" regulation of speech. But the Court recognised that in principle their symbolic acts enjoyed the protection of the First Amendment. Justice Marshall, in a perceptive dissent, said:

> "A disquieting feature of this case is that it lends credence to the idea that judicial administration of the First Amendment, in conjunction with a social order marked by large disparities in wealth and other sources of power, tends systematically to discriminate against efforts by the relatively disadvantaged to convey their political ideas."[85]

It is just that systematic inequality in the actual enjoyment of human rights which our courts too should strive to avoid.[86]

To conclude, I hope that the myths surrounding human rights can be dispelled as we approach the new millennium, so that lawyers will be encouraged either as practitioners or as scholars to make rights effective for everyone – to use technical expertise as the servant of imagination, for, if imagination without technique is futile, technique without imagination is barren.[87]

---

[82] This period is sometimes called the "Lochner era" after *Lochner* v. *New York* 198 US 45 (1905) in which the Supreme Court struck down a regulation limiting the hours of labour in bakeries to ten per day or sixty per week. Oliver Wendell Holmes famously dissented.

[83] 383 US 131 (1966).

[84] 468 US 288 (1984) at 306.

[85] *Ibid* at 305–6, n.14.

[86] See further on what I have called the "indirect regulation of speech" *infra* chapter 4.

[87] For a similarly optimistic view about what might flow from enactment of a Bill of Rights, see R Dworkin, *A Bill of Rights for Britain*, *supra* n. 27 at 23: "University law courses and faculties might develop . . . trying to produce a legal profession that could be the conscience, not just the servant, of government and industry. Different men and women might then be tempted to the law as a career, and from their ranks a more committed and idealistic generation of judges might emerge, encouraging a further cycle in the renaissance of liberty."

4

The Indirect Regulation of Speech: A Time and a Place for Everything?

There is increasing concern, not only among lawyers, that the foundations of freedom of speech in English law are insecure. Sometimes this concern has found expression in calls for a guaranteed right to freedom of speech, such as the one contained in the Constitution of the United States.[1] Much of the discussion has been about what I shall call "direct" regulation of speech, that is those rules of law which are obviously aimed at speech. Examples would include the rules relating to defamation and to breach of confidence. There are, however, numerous rules which, although not obviously aimed at speech, can still indirectly have the effect of hindering or prohibiting its exercise. Included among these would be rules prohibiting trespass to land,[2] obstruction of the highway and criminal damage. It is this neglected type of "indirect" regulation of speech that is the focus of this chapter.[3]

The primary purpose of this chapter is to explore the impact of recognising a right to freedom of speech on such indirect regulation of speech. I hope that this is useful because it is a way of testing in a particular context what, if any, will be the practical impact of enacting a Bill of Rights in this country.[4] So much energy has been spent in the United Kingdom for the last thirty

---

[1] The First Amendment states: "Congress shall make no law . . . abridging the freedom of speech . . ." According to judicial interpretation, it binds not only Congress but also the executive branch (for example *Clark* v. *Community for Creative Non-Violence* 468 US 288 (1984)) and the judicial branch (for example *New York Times* v. *United States* 403 US 713 (1971)) of the federal government. Furthermore, it also binds the states, through the Due Process clause of the Fourteenth Amendment (for example *Gitlow* v. *New York* 268 US 652 (1925)). See also Article 10 of the ECHR, which guarantees the right to freedom of expression, and Article 11, which guarantees the right to freedom of assembly.

[2] Now this would include the offence of trespassory assembly under sections 14A and 14B of the Public Order Act 1986, as amended.

[3] The distinction I make in this chapter is similar to the distinction between direct and indirect discrimination. It is well-established in UK law as well as in the United States and in European Community law that an act of discrimination on (for example) the grounds of race or sex may occur either directly or indirectly, because, although it may not be the purpose, that is the effect. See section 1 of the Sex Discrimination Act 1975; section 1 of the Race Relations Act 1976; Article 2 of Directive 76/207/EEC (the Directive on Equal Treatment between Men and Women in the field of Employment); and cases such as *Perera* v. *Civil Service Commission* [1983] ICR 428; *Mandla* v. *Dowell-Lee* [1983] 2 AC 548. Case C–170/84 *Bilka-Kaufaus GmbH* v. *Weber von Hartz* [1986] ECR 1607 (ECJ); Case C–127/92 *Enderby* v. *Frenchay Health Authority* [1994] ICR 112 (ECJ).

[4] On enacting a Bill of Rights, see *supra* Chapter 2.

years on the debate about whether we should have a Bill of Rights that, now at last we may have one, it is important to see how it would make a difference in practical contexts.

In this chapter I consider the principles of American constitutional law on the topic and try to suggest improvements on that American experience. This is not an exercise in comparative law as such, because knowledge of the current state of English law is, on the whole, taken for granted.[5] I hope, however, that the lessons for English law will become apparent from the exposition and critique of American law.

A word of explanation is due on why American law is used as a starting-point for this exercise. It is certainly not in the simplistic hope that doctrines can be translated from one set of social, political and constitutional systems to another. But American law does represent one, relatively mature, attempt to think consistently about what freedom of speech entails.[6] More importantly perhaps, American law illustrates the truth that determination of the scope of a legal right to freedom of speech requires reference to the extra-legal theories which explain and justify that right. Those theories can be summarised in five categories, which flow from the following concepts: personal autonomy; the search for truth; participatory democracy; equality; and the safety-valve.[7] Since such theories are applicable to all liberal-democratic societies, it is reasonable to suppose that the scope of freedom of speech should be at least as wide in any other system which seeks to emulate American law by guaranteeing that freedom.

DIRECT AND INDIRECT REGULATION

The distinction between direct and indirect regulation of speech can be clarified by the use of two specific examples.

First, there may be a rule which makes it an offence to advocate violation of the criminal law. This rule directly regulates speech, because its aim is

---

[5] A useful comparative work is E Barendt, *Freedom of Speech* (Oxford, Clarendon Press, 1985) (revised in reprints, the latest of which was published in 1996), which examines not only English and American law but German and European human rights law too.

[6] Cf. the jurisprudence on the European Convention on Human Rights, which seems rarely to have considered the impact of Article 10's guarantee of freedom of expression on indirect regulation: see JES Fawcett, *Application of the European Convention on Human Rights* 2nd edn (Oxford, Clarendon Press, 1987) at 252. In application 7215/75, 19 DR 66, the Commission held that the "physical expression of feelings" in a homosexual relationship was not covered by the Article, but this should not be regarded as the last word on the subject.

[7] All these theories can be found in the impressively concise formulation of Brandeis J, concurring in *Whitney* v. *California* 274 US 357, (1927), at 375–6 which includes the following: "Believing in the power of reason as applied through public discussion, they [those who won American independence] eschewed silence coerced by law – the argument of force in its worst form." See, for the first three theories, Barendt, *supra*, n.5, at 8–23. Of course, no single theory will suffice: "Any adequate conception of freedom of speech must . . . draw upon several strands of theory, in order to protect a rich variety of expressional modes," L Tribe, *American Constitutional Law* 2nd edn, (Mineola, New York, Foundation Press, 1988) at 789.

speech and nothing but speech. It will be noted that, moreover, this rule does not target all speech but a specific type of speech because of its meaning or content. For that reason, such a rule is called, in American terminlogy, a "content-based" regulation. It can be illustrated in diagrammatic form, as in Figure 1.

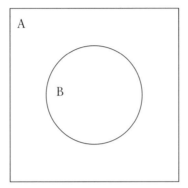

FIGURE 1 A = Scope of speech   B = scope of rule

Since such a regulation is a direct attack on the theories underlying freedom of speech (since B in Figure 1 is a sub-set of A), it is easy to see why such a rule should be viewed with suspicion: "By definition, content-based restrictions distort public debate in a content-differential manner . . . Such a law mutilates the 'thinking process of the community' and is thus incompatible with the central precepts of [freedom of speech]."[8] That is not to say that it cannot be legitimate. For to say that freedom of speech should be a right is not to say that it should be absolutely protected. As Ronald Dworkin has suggested, someone committed to a fundamental right such as freedom of speech can nevertheless permit it to be overridden "when necessary to protect the rights of others, or to prevent a catastrophe, or even to obtain a clear and major public benefit . . . What he cannot do is to say that the Government is justified in overriding a right on the minimal grounds that would be sufficient if no such right existed."[9] Metaphorically, one might describe freedom of speech as a zone of action protected by a high, but not insurmountable, wall.

The above criminal advocacy law may be contrasted with a criminal damage law. Such a law is not, on its face, aimed at speech at all. And yet, some speech may still be caught by its application. Take the example of writing on

[8] G Stone, "Content-Neutral Restrictions" (1987) 54 U. Chi. L. Rev. 46, 55.

[9] R Dworkin, *Taking Rights Seriously* (London, Duckworth, 1977) at 191–2. See also J Waldron, *Theories of Rights* (Oxford, OUP, 1984) at 15 for some views on what the "special force" of rights could be.

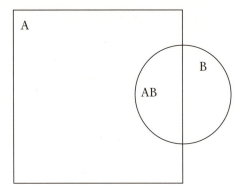

FIGURE 2 A = Scope of speech   B = scope of rule   AB = overlap between A and B

property belonging to another.[10] This kind of indirect regulation may be illustrated, again in diagrammatic form, as in Figure 2.

It will be apparent from Figure 2 that, in the case of indirect regulation, the problem for freedom of speech is not whether the rule itself is legitimate, but whether it may legitimately be applied in the overlap area marked "AB" in Figure 2. If the concept of a right as a zone of action protected by a high wall is retained, then it should follow that the state may not enter that zone even when it is enforcing an otherwise legitimate rule – unless, of course, it can get over the wall with the good reasons that are required whenever a direct regulation of speech is attempted.

This logical outcome is also supported by the theories underlying freedom of speech. Those theories are not dependent on the type of regulation: they focus on the right. Any other outcome would allow distortion of the democratic process and interference with the search for truth. It would close off an important safety-valve for unconventional ideas and eccentric media of communication. Furthermore, it would violate the principle of autonomy. For it is arguable that a person's freedom of speech includes the right to receive and impart information "either orally, in writing or in print, or in the form of art, or through any other media of his choice".[11]

Finally, and perhaps most neglected, any other outcome would violate the equality principle. This is because, while direct regulation tends to be aimed at the traditional media of the rich and powerful, indirect regulation often attacks the speech of the poor and powerless: "The idea that speech by large

[10] Current English law seems so blind to the fact that speech may be implicated in such conduct that in *Hardman* v. *Chief Constable of Avon and Somerset* [1986] Crim.L.R. 330, the only point of contention was whether the use of paint that was washable could constitute "damage" within the meaning of the Criminal Damage Act 1971 (held, it could). But note *infra*, n.22 and also the following newspaper item: "CND makes legal history with court nod for symbolic action", *The Guardian*, 18 February 1988, at 4.

[11] Article 19(2), International Covenant on Civil and Political Rights (ratified by the United Kingdom in 1976).

numbers of actively participating people should be given less protection than a barrage of published or broadcast material . . . has an obvious, perverse impact on the prospects for realising the ideal of one person, one voice."[12] As I have mentioned in Chapter 3, Marshall J once remarked:

> "A disquieting feature of this case is that it lends credence to the idea that judicial administration of the First Amendment, in conjunction with a social order marked by large disparities in wealth and other sources of power, tends systematically to discriminate against efforts by the relatively disadvantaged to convey their political ideas."[13]

That the indirect regulation of speech can occur even without being recognised as such makes it more, not less, suspect, because it can violate the principle of equality while appearing to maintain it.[14]

THE AMERICAN EXPERIENCE

American constitutional law does not employ the distinction made in this article between direct and indirect regulation of speech.[15] Instead, it adopts a similar distinction, based on the following typology of rules:

(1) content-based restrictions on speech;
(2) regulations of conduct which incidentally affect speech;
(3) content-neutral (or "time, place and manner") restrictions.

---

[12] L Tribe, *Constitutional Choices* (Cambridge, Massachusetts: Harvard University Press, 1985) at 199–200.

[13] *Clark* v. *Community for Creative Non-Violence* 468 US 288 (1984), at 305–6, n. 14.

[14] In this book I have suggested that the principle of equality is at the heart of human rights and that it requires substantive protection, not merely formal protection: see *supra* Introduction and Chapter 3. Sometimes substantive protection of the principle of equality may require the state to intervene in the market-place of ideas, so that some people's voices are not silenced: see generally O Fiss, *The Irony of Free Speech* (Cambridge, Massachusetts, Harvard University Press, 1996). It has to be said that the approach of the US courts has been even more formalistic in the last decade than it was when I first wrote the article on which this chapter is based. In this they seem to be out of tune with the more generally accepted approach in international human rights treaties and in jurisdictions such as Canada, which recognise that certain kinds of speech – such as racist speech which constitutes "group hate" speech – not only may, but should, be denied protection because they violate the right of minorities to be members of a polity who are entitled to equal concern and respect. See C McCrudden, "Freedom of Speech and Racial Equality" in P Birks (ed.) *Criminal Justice and Human Rights* (Oxford, OUP, 1995); Article 20(2) of the International Covenant on Civil and Political Rights (1966) and Article 4 of the Convention on the Elimination of All Forms of Racial Discrimination (1966); *R* v. *Keegstra* [1990] 3 SCR 697.

[15] It does, however, acknowledge the distinction between direct and indirect discrimination, to which the distinction I am making is similar: see, for example, *Griggs* v. *Duke Power Co* 401US 424 (1971). That was a case on the interpretation of the Civil Rights Act of 1964, and inspired the Sex Discrimination Act 1975 and the Race Relations Act 1976 in the UK. In contrast, when it comes to the *constitutional* right to equal protection of the laws, in the Fourteenth Amendment, the US Supreme Court has held that it prohibits only direct, and not indirect, discrimination: see *Washington* v. *Davis* 426 US 229 (1976).

I will suggest later that this classification is confusing, unnecessary and should be replaced by a more informative one. But, for the moment, I shall try to describe the current state of American law.[16]

(1) Content-based restrictions

In spite of the apparently emphatic language of the First Amendment's prohibition on laws abridging the freedom of speech, the Supreme Court has always stated that even content-based restrictions may be constitutionally valid. Because they attack the core rationales of freedom of speech, however, such restrictions are subjected to "strict scrutiny". This standard of judicial review requires that the restriction should be "narrowly tailored" to serve a "compelling governmental interest". The theoretical concept of a right as a zone of action protected by high wall, which may in exceptional circumstances be surmounted, is thus mirrored, in legal doctrine, in this formula.[17]

In *Brandenburg* v. *Ohio*,[18] for example, the Supreme Court stated that a criminal advocacy law of the type mentioned above would be valid provided it embraced only those situations "where such advocacy is directed to inciting or producing imminent lawless action and is likely to incite or produce such action". This is because the government has a "compelling" interest in preventing lawless action once it has become imminent, and because the requirements of intention and likelihood make the restriction on speech no greater than necessary to serve that interest.

The English common law has no counterpart to strict scrunity, although it has been persuasively argued that it does sometimes accord freedom of speech the status of a "public interest", to be weighed in the balance against other public interests.[19] But, where such an interest has been discovered, it has usually been in the context of content-based restrictions only.[20] The following

---

[16] See generally R Rotunda and J Nowak, *Constitutional Law* 5th edn (St Paul, Minnesota, West Publishing, 1995) ch. 16.

[17] As I have suggested earlier in this book, this is very similar to the concepts of "pressing social need" and "proportionality" which are used in the jurisprudence on the European Convention on Human Rights: see *supra* Chapter 3. The US concept of "intermediate scrutiny" (which I outline later in this chapter) is also an example of proportionality. My suggestion in this and other chapters is that there should be a flexible, "sliding scale" concept of proportionality which is sensitive to different contexts but not a rigid demarcation between different standards of scrutiny.

[18] 395 US 444, 447 (1969). This is the modern formulation of the famous "clear and present danger" test introduced by Holmes J in *Schenck* v. *United States* 249 US 47 (1919).

[19] Since the article on which this chapter is based first appeared, this has been confirmed in cases such as *Derbyshire CC* v. *Times Newspapers Ltd* [1993] AC 534; *R* v. *Advertising Standards Authority, ex p. Vernon Pools Organisation Ltd* [1992] 1 WLR 1289 (Laws J); *Prebble* v. *Television New Zealand Ltd* [1995] 1 AC 321 at 336 (Lord Browne-Wilkinson). See further on the common law's capacity to protect human rights *supra* Chapters 1 and 3.

[20] See A Boyle, "Freedom of Expression as a Public Interest in English law" [1982] PL 574 at 575: "The most obvious type of case where the issue arises in this way concerns press reporting which is alleged to be in contempt of court, but actions for breach of confidence, breach of copyright

two types of *indirect* regulation are not generally thought to raise freedom of speech problems in this country.[21]

(2) Regulations of conduct which incidentally affect speech

This category comprises "general" laws, which appear to have nothing to do with speech but which can still obstruct its exercise because it can be characterised as criminal damage, trespass to land, etc.

One reason why such rules have received so little scrutiny, at least in the UK, as restrictions on speech is that they play on an intuitive distinction between "speech" and "conduct".[22] After all, freedom of speech is only a special principle to the extent that speech is special.[23] Otherwise, the principle would collapse into a general one, that of personal autonomy. In fact, however, it is possible to be consistent and to say both that "speech" is especially important and that it should be construed more broadly than merely verbal activity, so as to include all expressive activity.

The intuitive distinction between speech and conduct breaks down, because all speech requires some conduct. Writing, printing and broadcasting are obvious examples. But even oral speech requires some muscular contraction to move the vocal chords and the tongue. Moreover, there are numerous, and powerful, examples of "symbolic speech": of these, displaying a flag is a familiar one, but burning one is no less symbolic.[24]

If the distinction between speech and conduct is discarded, then how is the protection of expressive activity to be limited? Will freedom of speech simply become a charter for law-breakers? Three options are available for a revised definition of "speech".

First, conduct could be regarded as speech whenever that is intended by the person engaged in it. But such an expansive definition may be ineffective in

or discovery of documents or information have increasingly shown some awareness that, there too, judges may have to protect freedom of information from disproprotionate encroachment." (footnotes omitted)

[21] For one of the refreshing exceptions, see *Hirst and Agu* v. *Chief Constable of West Yorks* (1986) 85 Cr App R 143 at 151 *per* Otton J: "The courts have long recognised the right to free speech to protest on matters of public concern" (in the context of whether reasonable use of the highway for leafleting was done with "lawful excuse" within the meaning of s.137, Highways Act 1980: held, it was). See further S Bailey, "Wilfully Obstructing the Freedom to Protest?" [1987] PL 495. Cf the way in which *Hirst* was distinguished in the context of "trespassory assembly" in *DPP* v. *Jones* [1997] 2 All ER 119 at 124b (McCowan LJ) and 126j (Collins J).

[22] See generally Barendt *supra* n.5 at 41–8.

[23] R Bork, "Neutral Principles and the First Amendment" (1971) 47 Indiana LJ 1, 25.

[24] The act of flag-burning was held (by a majority of five judges to four) to be an act of symbolic speech protected by the First Amendment in *Texas* v. *Johnson* 491 US 397 (1989). The ensuing public outcry led Congress to enact the Flag Protection Act of 1989, which provided that "[w]hoever knowingly mutilates, defaces, physically defiles, burns, maintains on the floor or ground, or tramples upon any flag of the United States" was liable to conviction. This Act was in turn held to be unconstitutional in *US* v. *Eichmann* 496 US 310 (1990) – again by a majority of five to four.

distinguishing sincere claims that a person was engaged in speech from insincere excuses by one who has been caught violating an otherwise legitimate rule.[25] Take the example of speed limits on the highway. How could one tell whether someone exceeded a speed limit to protest at state paternalism (or to make some other statement)? While even something as abhorrent as a political assassination can be understood as speech (although it need not be protected speech),[26] speeding is not thus understood – at least as our society stands at the present time. This could change, especially if lots of protesters exceeded a speed limit, became "martyrs" and hit the headlines. But that just goes to show that communication is not a unilateral act; it is an interpersonal process. Activity is expressive not merely because it is intended to be, but because it can also be understood to be, expressive.

The second way to define speech is, therefore, to require that conduct be understood as speech by other people. So as to avoid problems of proof, this could be framed as an objective test: the activity must be reasonably capable of being understood as an expressive one. But, if this test were adopted in isolation, it would be open to abuse by the person who does not sincerely intend to make a statement by engaging in the conduct.

The final and, I suggest, the best way of identifying speech is, therefore, to require that it should both be intended to be expressive and be reasonably capable of being understood as such. This was, in fact, the test reached in the American case in which the question was most clearly addressed by the Supreme Court, *Clark* v. *Community for Creative Non-Violence*.[27] It should be noted that the objective limb of this test does not preclude novel media of expression, provided only that they can reasonably be so understood. In *Clark*, Marshall J remarked that: ". . . sitting or standing in a library is a commonplace activity . . . However, for Negroes to stand or sit in a 'whites only' library in Louisiana in 1965 was powerfully expressive; in that particular context, those acts became 'monuments of protest' against segregation."[28]

But even the test reached so far does not include all conduct which a proper respect for freedom of speech requires. Although, as the quotation from Marshall J. indicates, standing can sometimes be speech, it usually is not. Yet often speech will not be possible unless a person can stand somewhere. When, for example, a person stands on the highway holding a placard, it would be meaningless to allow him or her to hold the placard but to impose an absolute prohibition on standing on the highway. The concept of speech must, there-

---

[25] "We cannot accept the view that an apparently limitless variety of conduct can be labeled 'speech' whenever the person engaged in the conduct intends thereby to express an idea": *United States* v. *O'Brien* 391 US 367, (1968), at 376 *per* Warren CJ.

[26] Cf. Barendt *supra*, n.5 at 43–4.

[27] 468 US 288 (1984).

[28] *Ibid.* at 306, referring to *Brown* v. *Louisiana* 383 US 131 (1966).

fore, be broad enough to include all conduct which, though not expressive in itself, is necessarily involved during the relevant expressive activity.[29]

The reluctance to admit such a wide concept of speech often rests on a fear that many legitimate interests will thereby be sacrificed. But such a fear should be dissipated as soon as it is realised that the mere recognition of conduct as speech is not to guarantee it absolute protection. It is only to guarantee it the protection that freedom of speech always deserves once one has made a commitment to accord it the status of a human right.

How are we to decide whether this second type of rule is consistent with freedom of speech? The leading American case on the question suggests that a "general" law which regulates conduct but incidentally affects speech, is to be subjected, not to "strict scrutiny", but to a lower, intermediate degree of scrutiny.

United States v. *O'Brien*[30] concerned the Universal Military Training and Service Act of 1948, as amended in 1965, under which an offence was committed by anyone "who forges, alters, knowingly destroys, knowingly mutilates, or in any manner changes any such [selective service] certificate". O'Brien was convicted because he had burned his certificate (his "draft card"). He had done it in a public place, on the steps of the South Boston Courthouse, with the intention "that other people would re-evaluate their positions with Selective Service, with the armed forces, and re-evaluate their place in the culture of today". Although the Supreme Court, speaking through Warren CJ, assumed that the communicative element in his conduct was "sufficient to bring into play the First Amendment", it went on to warn that "it does not necessarily follow that the destruction of a registration certificate is constitutionally protected activity." In deciding whether it was, the Court laid down three criteria which a rule regulating conduct but incidentally affecting speech must satisfy before it may be upheld as consistent with the First Amendment:

(i)   it must further "an important or substantial governmental interest" (but note that the interest need not be "compelling");

(ii) the incidental restriction on First Amendment freedoms must be "no greater than is essential to the furtherance of that interest";

(iii) the interest must be "unrelated to the suppression of free expression".[31]

(This third criterion is crucial, for otherwise the restriction would be "content-based" and therefore subject to all the severity of "strict scrutiny".)

The fact that this test represents a lesser degree of scrutiny than "strict

---

[29] Indeed this is why human rights charters usually guarantee freedom of assembly as well as freedom of expression: both are set out in the First Amendment to the US Constitution and Article 11 of the European Convention on Human Rights protects freedom of assembly. The two rights are clearly complementary but not identical.

[30] 391 US 367 (1968).

[31] *Ibid.* at 377.

scrutiny" is indicated by the outcome of *O'Brien* itself. For while governmental action is almost invariably struck down by the US Supreme Court if subjected to strict scrutiny, it was held that all three criteria were met, so that O'Brien's conviction was constitutional.

It will be evident from the outcome of the case that the three criteria were used not merely to uphold the validity of the rule in question, but also to permit it to be applied to a person who, it was conceded, was engaged in expressive activity. If the Court's reasoning is correct, it would follow that, in Figure 2 above, if the validity of the rule B could be established, then it could applied in the area marked "AB". I would suggest that such reasoning, which fails to distinguish between striking down a rule altogether and preventing its application inside a protected zone of action, is flawed by a fundamental error of logic. I will come back to this error again, after discussion of the American treatment of "content-neutral" restrictions.

(3) Content-neutral restrictions[32]

Even if "speech" is given a broad meaning, to include all expressive activity, the conclusion can surely not be that no regulation of speech is permissible.[33] This is because, first, the principle of "universalisability" requires each of us to accord to every other person the same right to speak freely as we demand for ourselves. Furthermore, there are other rights and interests which may need accommodation: for example, the interest in being free of noise at certain hours in residential districts. Such an interest brings us then to "content-neutral" restrictions on speech, which regulate the time, place or manner of speech. Although such a regulation may appear on its face to be concerned with speech, it is not concerned with the meaning of what is said but only with the location, the decibel level, and so on. How are we to decide whether such a restriction is consistent with freedom of speech? Again, American law provides a useful starting-point, although (as I shall suggest) it has shortcomings.

In *Clark* v. *Community for Creative Non-Violence*,[34] a permit was granted to conduct a wintertime demonstration on two sites in Washington DC (LaFayette Park and The Mall), one of which is close to the White House and

---

[32] Since the article on which this chapter is based was first published, it has become clear that the US courts will distinguish between two different types of content-neutral restrictions. They will give greater scrutiny to content-neutral *injunctions* than to *statutes*: see, for example, *Madsen* v. *Women's Health Center Inc* 114 S Ct 2516 (1994).

[33] Even someone associated with an "absolutist" view of the First Amendment, at least in respect of *political* speech, readily agreed that when "self-governing men demand freedom of speech they are not saying that every individual has an inalienable right to speak whenever, wherever, however he chooses": A Meiklejohn, *Political Freedoms: The Constitutional Powers of the People* (New York: OUP, 1948), at 25.

[34] *Supra* n. 28.

the other to the Capitol, to draw attention to the plight of the homeless. But in granting the permit, the National Park Service refused permission to sleep on the sites because, although they were national parks, they were not designated campgrounds. The Supreme Court held, by a majority of seven to two, that, even assuming that sleeping could in that context constitute speech, the prohibition on camping in non-designated areas could constitutionally be made a condition for the granting of a permit.

In delivering the Court's opinion, White J stated that "expression, whether oral or written or symbolized by conduct, is subject to reasonable time, place and manner restrictions." He laid down four criteria[35] for determining the reasonableness of such restrictions:

(i)   The restriction must be "justified without reference to the content of the regulated speech" (otherwise, of course, it would not be "content-neutral").
(ii) It must serve a "significant" governmental interest.
(iii) It must be narrowly tailored to serve that interest.
(iv) It must leave open "ample alternative channels for communication of the information".[36]

It will be evident that the first three criteria represent, in essence, the same test as the one in *O'Brien* to determine the validity of rules falling into category (2) above.[37] But the fourth criterion requires further comment. For one thing, it raises important questions about what "ample" alternatives are, and in whose opinion; it may, indeed, contradict a famous dictum in an earlier case.[38] More fundamentally, the Court makes the assumption that one can detach "the" information being transmitted from the particular channel chosen by the speaker herself or himself. This assumption is contradicted not only

---

[35] *Ibid.* at 293.

[36] The test for content-neutral restrictions is sometimes formulated differently. For example, in *US Postal Service* v. *Council of Greenburgh* 453 US 114 (1981) the court spoke of "adequate" alternative channels of communication; and in *City of Renton* v. *Playtime Theaters Inc* 475 US 41 (1986) the court held that the restriction should not "unreasonably limit" alternative channels of communication.

[37] The difficulty in drawing a line between the two categories is illustrated by *Barnes* v. *Glen Theater Inc* 501 US 560 (1991), the case about nude dancing. A majority of the US Supreme Court held that an Indiana statute prohibiting the knowing or intentional appearing in a public place in a state of nudity could constitutionally be applied so as to require female dancers to wear (as a minimum) "pasties" and a G-string. Rehnquist CJ, who wrote the plurality Opinion for the Court, said that the time, place and manner test and the *O'Brien* test are much the same. Scalia J concurred in the result but would go further than any other Supreme Court Justice to date in that he regards such regulations as being outside the scope of the First Amendment altogether because they are not specifically directed at expression, i.e. he disagrees in effect with the central thesis of this essay that indirect regulation of speech can violate the right to freedom of expression.

[38] "One is not to have his liberty of expression in appropriate places abridged on the plea that it may be exercised in some other place": *Schneider* v. *State (Town of Irvington)* 308 US 147, 163 (1939), *per* Roberts J.

by the evidence of socio-linguistics,[39] but also by the Court's acknowledgement, on an earlier occasion, that the medium is often the message: "... much linguistic expression serves a dual communicative function: it conveys not only ideas capable of relatively precise, detached exposition, but otherwise inexplicable emotions as well."[40] In *Clark* itself, sleeping in wintertime near the "magisterial residence of the President of the United States" lent a peculiar poignancy to the protest which "even Dickens could not match".[41] In fact there was, as Marshall J noted in dissent, "a remarkably apt fit between the activity in which [the demonstrators] seek to engage and the social problem they seek to highlight".[42]

In spite of the outcome in *Clark*, the majority opinion indicates that even when speech is caught by time, place and manner restrictions, the principle of freedom of speech cannot simply be ignored under the US Constitution.[43] Moreover, the dissenters' disagreement with the majority lay not in the formulation of the appropriate criteria, but in their application. In particular, they felt that the Court was unduly deferential to the executive's own assessment of whether the four criteria were met. The Court's "minimal scrutiny" led Marshall J to express doubts about the desirability of the "two-tiered" approach to freedom of speech cases: "By narrowly limiting its concern to see whether a given regulation creates a content-based restriction, the Court has seemingly overlooked the fact that content-neutral restrictions are also capable of unnecessarily restricting protected expressive activity."[44]

I would suggest that the approach of the Court criticised by Marshall J is not only undesirable, but also unnecessary. It has earned a respectability, even among liberals, only because the Court has failed to distinguish between a challenge to the rule itself and the contention that the rule may not be applied to a particular situation: "it is evident from our cases that the validity of this regulation need not be judged solely by reference to the demonstration at hand."[45]

This error of logic also occurs, as was noted above, when American law considers rules falling into category (2) above. It is interesting, therefore, to see that the same error is not (or, at least, was not in the past) repeated in the context of freedom of religion, which is protected by the same First Amendment that guarantees freedom of speech.[46] In that context, rules which

---

[39] H Tajfel & C Fraser (eds) *Introducing Social Psychology* (Harmondsworth, Penguin, 1978) ch. 5.

[40] *Cohen v. California* 403 US 15, 26 (1971), *per* Harlan J.

[41] *Per* Judge Edwards, concurring, when the case was in the court below: *sub nom* CCNV v. *Watt* 703 F. 2d. 596, 601.

[42] 468 US 288, 305–6.

[43] "One could imagine a constitutional system in which such governmental behaviour would automatically be upheld, however devastating its consequences for freedom of expression . . . That is not our system . . ."; Tribe *supra* n. 7 at 978.

[44] 468 US 288, 313.

[45] *Ibid.* at 297 (White J).

[46] "Congress shall make no law respecting an establishment of religion, or prohibiting the free exercise thereof nor abridging the freedom of speech . . ."

are otherwise valid are not permitted to interfere with the free exercise of religion, subject to the exceptional circumstances permitted by strict scrutiny.

In *Wisconsin* v. *Yoder*,[47] for example, the Supreme Court held that a law requiring parents to send children to school until the age of sixteen, though valid, could not constitutionally be applied to the defendants, who were members of the Amish faith and who refused to send their children, aged fourteen and fifteen, to school after the eighth grade. Speaking for six of the seven members of the Court who heard the case, Burger CJ said: ". . . only those interests of the highest order and those not otherwise served can overbalance legitimate claims to the free exercise of religion."[48] Applying that test, which requires strict scrutiny, the Court found that the law was not narrowly tailored to serve "interests of the highest order".

> "The record strongly indicates that accommodating the religious objections of the Amish by forgoing one, or at most two, additional years of compulsory education will not . . . materially detract from the welfare of society . . . [W]e cannot accept a parens patriae claim of such all-encompassing scope and with such sweeping potential for broad and unforeseeable application as that urged by the State."[49]

Another, perhaps more controversial, example is provided by the decision of the Supreme Court of California in *People* v. *Woody*.[50] Speaking through Tobriner J, the Court held that, since the defendant, a member of the Navajo tribe, had used a prohibited drug called peyote

> "in a bona fide pursuit of a religious faith, and since the practice does not frustrate a *compelling* interest of the State, the *application* of the statute improperly defeated the immunity of the First Amendment of the Constitution of the United States."[51]

The emphasised words make it plain that an otherwise valid law may not be applied inside a constitutionally protected zone of action unless the rigours of strict scrutiny are satisfied.

In more recent case law, the US Supreme Court has moved away from its more logical approach in *Wisconsin* v. *Yoder* and has in effect overruled *People* v. *Woody*. In *Employment Division* v. *Smith*,[52] which also concerned the sacramental use of peyote by Native Americans, the Court held that all "incidental burdens" on the free exercise of religion which are imposed by neutral laws are constitutional. The case concerned two individuals who were disqualified from receiving unemployment compensation benefits under a state law that disqualified anyone who had been dismissed on the ground of job-related misconduct. They had been dismissed as drug and alcohol abuse rehabilitation counsellors at a private clinic after it was found that they had

---

[47] 406 US 205 (1972).
[48] *Ibid.* at 215.
[49] *Ibid.* at 234.
[50] 40 Cal. Rptr 69 (1964).
[51] *Ibid.* at 71 (*emphasis added*).
[52] 494 US 872 (1990).

ingested peyote which was banned under state law. In his Opinion for the majority of the Court, Scalia J did recognise that there were exceptions to the general principle enunciated in *Smith*. One exception, he said, was provided by those "hybrid" cases where both free exercise and other constitutional rights were involved: he placed *Wisconsin* v. *Yoder* in this category.[53] What is instructive for other jurisdictions (like the United Kingdom) that may wish to learn from American experience is that, following *Smith*, which was severely criticised, Congress enacted the Religious Freedom Restoration Act of 1993, which provides significant statutory (but not, of course, constitutional) protection against incidental burdens on the free exercise of religion. The Act provides that the government shall not substantially burden a person's exercise of religion even if the burden results from a rule of general applicability unless the burden imposed is narrowly tailored to serve a compelling interest. This is, as we have seen, the language of strict scrutiny. In this instance, therefore, I would suggest that the United Kingdom would do better to learn from the *earlier* case-law of the US courts, and the Act of Congress which reflects that case-law, rather than to follow the more recent case-law.

AN ALTERNATIVE SCHEME

It has been seen that American law classifies rules according to three types: content-based restrictions; regulations of conduct which incidentally affect speech; and content-neutral restrictions. While restrictions of the first type are subjected to strict scrutiny, restrictions of the second and third types are subjected to variants of a lesser scrutiny, sometimes called "intermediate scrutiny". I would suggest that this scheme for the protection of freedom of speech can be improved in two ways. First, the classification can be replaced by one that is more illuminating. Secondly, the rigid two tiers of scrutiny[54] can be replaced by a single, but flexible, standard of strict scrutiny.[55]

---

[53] 494 US at 881.

[54] In fact there is a third, low level of scrutiny, reserved (perhaps illogically) for some categories of speech, such as obscenity and "fighting words", deemed to be of no social value (see, for example, *Chaplinsky* v. *New Hampshire* 315 US 368, 371–2 (1942), *per* Murphy J, though that case should now be contrasted with *RAV* v. *St Paul* 505 US 377 (1992) which concerned "hate speech" laws and which has virtually distinguished *Chaplinsky* out of existence) and for those government-owned places that are not by tradition or designation "public forums" (*Perry Education Assn* v. *Perry Local Education Assn* 460 US 37, 46 (1983), *per* White J).

[55] One motive for a tiered approach may be that strict scrutiny would otherwise invalidate the regulation, because it is applied mechanistically. *Cf.* a similar criticism of the case-law on the Equal Protection clause of the Fourteenth Amendment, where a tiered analysis is "viewed by many as a result-oriented substitute for more critical analysis": *Craig* v. *Boren* 429 US 190, 210 (1976), *per* Powell J, concurring.

(1) A new classification

The distinction made in American law between content-based and other restrictions is simplistic and too obscure.[56] It could be replaced with the following classification of rules which affect the exercise of freedom of speech.

(a) Some rules discriminate not against all speech but against a particular viewpoint. Such discrimination should be the most difficult, if not impossible, to justify. This is because it denies the premises which lie at the core of the theories underlying freedom of speech, in particular the theory based on equality. Indeed "viewpoint discrimination" reduces the concept of freedom of speech from the status of a right to that of a licence: "Freedom of speech is indivisible; unless we protect it for all, we will have it for none."[57] Of course, sometimes the search for equality will justify the state in prohibiting certain kinds of speech which is used as a verbal weapon to attack vulnerable minorities: they are entitled as members of a political community to equal concern and respect and not to be singled out for hate speech.[58]

(b) Another type of rule is that which, while it does not discriminate between viewpoints, does remove an entire subject from discussion from any viewpoint. This type of restriction should again be very difficult to justify, although one can think of obvious examples (for example, information revealing the movement of soldiers in wartime)[59] where such a restriction might satisfy strict scrutiny. But ordinarily the equality principle should provide a floor, not a ceiling, to the protection of freedom of speech: government should not be able to escape its rigour by excluding a subject from discussion altogether.[60]

[56] For one thing, it is difficult to distinguish between a regulation of conduct affecting speech and a content-neutral regulation of speech. In *Clark, supra* n. 35, the rule against camping in non-designated areas could have been treated as a rule governing conduct but affecting speech, although the Court chose to view it as a content-neutral restriction on speech. Both types are, it is submitted, just examples of "indirect" regulation of speech.

[57] H Kalven, "Upon Rereading Mr Justice Black on the First Amendment" (1967) 14 UCLA L Rev. 428, 437. See also Karst, "Equality as a Central Principle in the First Amendment" (1975) 43 U. Chi.L.Rev. 20.

[58] In this respect the US case-law such as *RAV* v. *St Paul* 505 US 377 (1992) should not be followed. Given the United Kingdom's traditions (including the fact that there are laws against incitement to racial hatred) it would be preferable to follow the approach of the Supreme Court of Canada in *R* v. *Keegstra* [1990] 3 SCR 697 and of international human rights treaties: for example, Article 20(2) of the International Covenant on Civil and Political Rights (1966) and Article 4 of the Convention on the Elimination of All Forms of Racial Discrimination (1966).

[59] The example given in *Near* v. *Minnesota* 283 US 697, 716 (1931).

[60] See, for example, *Police Dept of Chicago* v. *Mosley* 408 US 92, 95–6 (1972), *per* Marshall J: ". . . government may not grant the use of a forum to people whose views it finds acceptable, but deny use to those wishing to express less favoured or more controversial views. And [further] it may not select which issues are worth discussing or debating in public facilities." For a recent example, see *Lamb's Chapel* v. *Center Moriches Union Free School District* 508 US 384 (1993). There a New York law allowed school boards to adopt regulations for the use of school

(c) Going one step further up the ladder of generality, there is a third type of restriction which is aimed at all speech, irrespective of the viewpoint or the subject. An example of such discrimination is provided by section 11 of the Public Order Act 1986, which requires advance notice of a procession if it has certain, only communicative, purposes.[61] Even if speech were of no special importance, surely it should not be especially disadvantaged.

(d) Finally, there are truly indirect regulations of speech, for each of the first three types is, in some sense, directly about speech, each singling out speech for special treatment. Since the purpose of indirect regulations is less likely to be inconsistent with the theories underlying freedom of speech, they will normally be easier to justify than any of the direct types of regulation. But, although improper purposes should be rooted out, it should not be forgotten that, in their effect, even indirect restrictions can violate the principles underlying freedom of speech.

(2) The Appropriate Degree of Protection

American law lowers the standard of scrutiny as soon as a rule is found not to be content-based. I would suggest that all restrictions on speech should be subjected to one standard of scrutiny. The wall surrounding the protected zone of action should not be lowered just because the state has chosen to attack it by a rule in indirect form. Of course, indirect entry into that zone may satisfy scrutiny more easily than direct assault, but the standard should remain constant. Whatever its form, no incursion should be permitted unless that is "necessary to serve a compelling interest".

"NECESSARY TO SERVE A COMPELLING INTEREST"

The requirement that every restriction on speech must, to be consistent with the notion of freedom of speech as a right, be "necessary to serve a compelling interest" contains within it the following three elements:

property at times when the school was not in session. The board in question authorised use of school property for social, civic or recreational uses and for uses by political organisations but denied it to a religious congregation. The US Supreme Court unanimously ruled that the regulation violated the free speech clause of the First Amendment. White J, in the majority Opinion, went further and said that this was an example of viewpoint discrimination, because the board would have permitted use of school property for discussion of issues such as family values which were *not* related to the views of a religious group.

[61] Under section 11(1), notice is required of a proposal to hold a public procession intended "to demonstrate support for or opposition to the views of any person or body of persons" or "to publicise a cause or campaign" or "to mark or commemorate an event." In America "[f]or the most part, the Court has taken a hard line on discrimination against communicative activity, although not nearly as hard a line as it has taken on content-based discrimination": Stone *supra* n. 9, at 101.

(i)   The countervailing interest must be not only legitimate and reasonable but compelling.

(ii)   The interest must be not just compelling in the abstract (for example the prevention of crime). It must be necessary to achieve that interest on the particular facts even at the expense of freedom of speech.[62]

(iii) The restriction must be no broader than necessary to achieve the countervailing interest.

It is sometimes suggested that formulae such as the one proposed here constitute no more than an invitation to "balance" freedom of speech against other interests. It is said by some to be an undesirable exercise.[63] It is said by others to be an impossible one.[64] Whatever the merits of balancing, it is submitted that the formula proposed does not permit straightforward balancing. Rather, it states that freedom of speech will prevail – unless it can be displaced for specific reasons which are articulable and clearly demonstrable. If that is balancing, then it is balancing which is weighted and structured.[65]

One way of structuring this judgment process is to take several specific factors into account. While none of the following may be dispositive, each (or several in combination) may help to decide whether the particular application of a rule is "necessary to serve a compelling interest".

(1) The target of the regulation

Although the standard of scrutiny should, unlike that in American law, remain constant, it may be more easily satisfied in the case of indirect regulation. For it is not the thesis of this chapter that the concerns underlying the American two-tiered approach are trivial.[66] An improper purpose should indeed render it more difficult to justify a restriction: far from being

---

[62] For the methodology of the European Court of Human Rights, see *Sunday Times* v. *United Kingdom* Series A. No. 30 (1979–80) 2 EHRR 245, 281: ". . . the Court's supervision under Article 10 covers not only the basic legislation but also the decision applying it . . . the Court has to be satisfied that the interference was necessary having regard to the facts and circumstances prevailing in the specific case before it" (footnotes omitted).

[63] For example, B Williams in Smart & Williams, *Utilitarianism: For and Against* (Cambridge, Cambridge University Press, 1973) at 93.

[64] For example, J Finnis, *Natural Law and Natural Rights* (Oxford, Clarendon Press, 1980) at 114.

[65] For an analysis of the structured way in which the European Court of Justice approaches the question of "proportionality" when fundamental rights protected by EC law are at stake, see G de Búrca, "The Principle of Proportionality and its Application in EC law" [1993] YBEL 105.

[66] For an important defence of the tiered approach, see Stone *supra* n. 9 especially at 57: "The three factors – distortion of public debate, improper motivation, and communicative impact – provide a sound basis for the Court's use of a strict standard of review to test the constitutionality of . . . content-based restrictions . . . Moroever, because these factors do not arise with the same frequency in content-neutral restrictions, they also explain why the Court does not employ a similarly strict standard to test [their] constitutionality."

compelling, such an interest would not even be legitimate. I am only suggesting that even indirect regulation should not unnecessarily restrict speech.

(2) The severity of the restriction

This factor affects both how weighty the countervailing interest must be to be compelling and how tight the nexus must be between the restriction and that interest to count as necessary. For instance, a total ban should require greater justification than the imposition of conditions, although the conditions should also be scrutinised to ensure that they do not amount to a ban. Similarly, an overbroad power to ban would not pass the requirement of necessity.

(3) The timing of the restriction

This factor has traditionally been regarded as going both to what is compelling and to what is necessary. In particular, restraints before the expressive activity has taken place are frowned upon even more than punishment of it:

> "The impact and consequences of subsequent punishment . . . are materially different from those of prior restraint. Prior restraint upon speech suppresses the precise freedom which the First Amendment sought to protect."[67]

Not everyone agrees that all prior restraints are necessarily worse than subsequent punishment, but this is not the place for a full appraisal of the rival views.[68] Suffice it to say that the distinction should not be applied automatically.

For one thing, it is not always easy to classify a restriction as prior or subsequent. This is particularly because there seems to be a third type of restriction: what might be called "the contemporaneous incapacitation". An example would be a power of summary arrest (which may, of course, never lead to a charge). While this seems to resemble subsequent punishment, its exercise may curtail a demonstration as effectively as any prior restraint.

Furthermore, every restriction needs to be examined to see if the particular components of the rationale behind the distaste for prior restraints are present in any specific case.[69] Of those components, special mention should be made of two. First, the effect of delay on speech: under a system of prior restraints, speech never reaches the market-place of ideas and, even if it does, it may well be obsolete stock. In distinguishing political speech from the "sub-

---

[67] *Carroll* v. *Commissioners of Princess Anne* 393 US 175, 181 (1968), *per* Fortas J.

[68] *Cf.* F Schauer, *Free Speech: A Philosophical Inquiry* (Cambridge, Cambridge University Press, 1982) at 148–52.

[69] For a list of seven of the defects of prior restraint, see T Emerson, "The Doctrine of Prior Restraint" (1955) 20 L. and Contem. Prob. 648, 656–60.

ject of sex [which] is of constant but rarely particularly topical interest", Harlan J once noted that a "delay of even a day or two may be of crucial importance in some instances."[70] Secondly, prior restraints can often be imposed without the procedural safeguards associated with a trial, such as the burden of proof. Indeed, "sensitive issues of free expression are decided largely by a minor bureaucrat [or even a police officer] rather than through an institution designed to secure a somewhat more independent, objective, and liberal judgment."[71]

(4) The location of the expressive activity

Owing to the laws of physics, each of us must have some relationship to land at all times. If, therefore, the mere ownership of property rights were always sufficient to exclude expressive activity, freedom of speech could never be exercised as of right, only by licence, except on one's own land. On the other hand, the concept of "property" may embrace interests which are, in a given case, sufficient to warrant protection at the expense of unrestricted speech, for example the interest in privacy in one's home.

The location of speech affects the necessity of a restriction. To take an example from a real American case, a prohibition on even silent vigils in a library may be broader than is necessary to secure the interest in silence.[72]

The location also affects whether a countervailing interest is compelling, especially since there are places which, by tradition or designation, are reserved for expressive activity.

> "[I]n an open, democratic society the streets, the parks and other public places are a public forum that the citizen can commandeer; the generosity and empathy with which such facilities are made available is an index of freedom."[73]

This legal concept gives a physical reality to the political concept of the "public forum", that realm of discussion which is vital for a people to be truly self-governing and for each citizen to be a truly free participant in the political community.

Although the location of speech in a conventional public forum should require an even stronger countervailing interest before it can be accepted as compelling, speech in unconventional places should still be protected by strict

---

[70] *A Quantity of Books* v. *Kansas* 376 US 205, 224 (1964). See also *New York Times* v. *United States* 403 US 713, 727 (1971), *per* Brennan J concurring: ". . . every restraint issued in this case . . . has violated the First Amendment – and not less so because that restraint was justified as necessary to afford the courts an opportunity to examine the claim more thoroughly." *Cf.* the approach of English law in *Att-Gen.* v. *Guardian Newspapers* [1987] 1 WLR 1248, especially Lord Brandon's speech.

[71] Emerson *supra* n. 70 at 658.

[72] *Brown* v. *Louisiana* 393 US 131 (1966).

[73] H Kalven, "The Concept of the Public Forum" [1965] S Ct Rev.1, 11–12.

scrutiny – but, of course, the standard is more likely to be met. Take, for example, a peace-camp at a nuclear base. The location, although not conventional, is peculiarly appropriate for that demonstration. The countervailing interest must be compelling (for example, the protection of national security) but, furthermore, it must be shown that nothing less than a total ban (for example, the reservation of a specific place for demonstrations) will achieve that interest.

(5) The width of discretion vested in the state

A legal system which is sensitive to freedom of speech should design systems of discretion which are controllable and reduce the chance of their abuse. In the context of freedom of speech in particular, discretion must not be too broad, because of the "chilling effect", which induces self-censorship.[74]

Moreover, the state should be accountable for the exercise of discretion in a particular case by having to show that that exercise is necessary to serve a compelling interest.

A CASE STUDY

The importance of the standard of scrutiny proposed above may become clearer from the study of a specific, hypothetical case.

Imagine that Gail is a pacifist who wishes to draw attention to the horrors of nuclear war on the anniversary of the dropping of the first "Bomb". On 6 August, she uses washable paint to draw "human shadows" on the pavement, to symbolise the shadows which alone, it is said, remained of some of those burnt to death at Hiroshima. This is speech because, on the test proposed above, it is intended to have, and is reasonably capable of being understood as having, communicative impact.

Gail is charged with an offence under section 1(1) of the Criminal Damage Act 1971, which states: "A person who without lawful excuse . . . damages any property belonging to another intending to . . . damage any such property . . . shall be guilty of an offence." Let us assume that, as the law now

---

[74] For example, *NAACP* v. *Button* 371 US 415, 433 (1963), *per* Brennan J: "Because First Amendment freedoms need breathing space to survive, government may regulate in the area only with narrow specificity." See also the works of Emerson, who for a long time has expressed concern at the problems of operating a system of freedom of speech, especially *supra* n. 70 at 658: "The function of the censor is to censor . . . He is often acutely responsive to interests which demand suppression . . . and not so well attuned to the more scattered and less aggressive forces which support free expression." See further *New York Times* v. *Sullivan* 376 US 254 (1964) for the importance of avoiding the "chilling effect", a phrase that was taken up in *Derbyshire County Council* v. *Times Newspapers Ltd* [1993] AC 534 at 548.

stands, Gail's conduct would satisfy all the elements of this offence.[75] What difference would it make if the law recognised that she was exercising her freedom of speech?

To apply the rule to Gail, the state must show that her conviction is necessary to serve a compelling interest. This contention can be examined in the light of the five factors outlined in the previous section.

First, the state benefits from the fact that the rule itself does not suffer from the defects of direct regulation of speech. But that is only the starting-point of the inquiry, not the end.

Secondly, the restriction is severe, almost total. The only place where Gail could paint the shadows would be on her own property, if she has any. In other words, if the restriction were automatically upheld, property rights would always prevail over freedom of speech.

Thirdly, the restriction does not suffer from the defects of prior restraint. But it should be remembered that the likelihood of successful prosecution in similar cases will affect whether such demonstrations are stopped in future. The outcome of this case may thus cause prior restraints in the future.

Fourthly, the location of the speech is the street, a traditional public forum. If Gail cannot "talk" to other citizens there, a major forum will be removed from the arena of discussion.

Fifthly, there is prosecutorial discretion. The state should have to show why this particular conviction is necessary to serve a compelling interest, when it is not thought necessary to convict the numerous pavement artists who frequent our shopping centres every Saturday.

On the other side, the state would point to the interest in property rights. But can such an interest really be compelling when all that is involved is a washable drawing, which will wash away with rain just as the pavement art does?

The outcome of a case such as this hypothetical one will depend on the exercise of judgment. For this reason, it is sometimes said that the legal formula is not as important as the personality and prejudices of the person whose judgment counts. But even if that is true, it may not be lost on people in Gail's position that often, though not always, the judgment will be exercised not by professional lawyers but by lay jurors or magistrates.[76]

---

[75] This assumption may be unwarranted if the interpretation placed on the words "lawful excuse" in the Highways Act 1980, s. 137 in *Hirst, supra* n. 22, can be placed by analogy on the same words in the Criminal Damage Act 1971.

[76] There should not, however, be complacency at the current composition of either juries or, in particular, the magistracy. But even a prominent radical lawyer felt able to say: "The theory of the lay magistracy has much to commend it . . . lay magistrates, if they were truly representative of the community in which they sit, would have many of the virtues of juries", T Gifford, *Where's the Justice?* (Harmondsworth, Penguin, 1986) at 37. For those "virtues" see *ibid.* ch. 5 and, generally, S H Bailey and M J Gunn, *The Modern English Legal System* 3rd edn (London, Sweet & Maxwell, 1996) at 192–213.

CONCLUSION

Freedom of speech is vital to individual human development and collective self-government:

"We act as we do because we communicate, not because we have drives and ideas first and then come together to express them. The self and society originate and develop *in* communication."[77]

The legal system of a free society should, therefore, give freedom of speech the status of a right: it shoud be a zone of action protected by a high wall, which the state may surmount only by meeting the standard of "strict scrutiny", by showing that a restriction on speech is "necessary to serve a compelling interest".

"Speech" should, as in American law, be read generously, to include all expressive activity: all conduct which is intended to have, and is reasonably capable of being understood as having, communicative impact. But the special protection afforded freedom of speech should not be reduced, as in American law, just because the form of the regulation of speech is indirect. In particular, the strictness of the scrutiny of applications of indirect regulations to speech should not be relaxed just because those regulations could be applied in non-speech contexts. Any other result is illogical as well as undesirable on the basis of the theories underlying freedom of speech.

Although strict scrutiny should not automatically be "fatal" scrutiny, the process of deciding whether a restriction is necessary to serve a compelling interest should be weighted and structured, not just an exercise in balancing in which freedom of speech could readily be traded off for other benefits.

While there will inevitably have to be reasonable regulation of the freedoms of expression and assembly, such regulation must not be allowed to go beyond what is necessary and so to strike at the core of those freedoms – at least for many people. While the time, place and manner of speech may be regulated, there must also be a time and a place for everything, including speech.

[77] H D Duncan, *Communication and Social Order* (New York, Bedminster Press, 1962) at 76.

5

The Protection of Privacy in English Public Law[1]

It is a truism that there is no right to privacy in English law. But then English law has historically not been comfortable with the idea of "rights" of any kind. It has preferred to concentrate on remedies.[2] In so far as the common law, and later equity, would grant a remedy to compensate for a legal wrong or to prevent the wrong occurring, it could be said that the plaintiff had a corresponding right. But, even understood in that sense, English law has not recognised privacy as an interest which would be protected so as to give rise to a cause of action. Privacy may be protected *indirectly* through other causes of action such as trespass to land, private nuisance and, perhaps most importantly, breach of confidence.[3] There is a serious debate which continues in the United Kingdom about whether that is a satisfactory state of affairs and whether, if it is not, some remedy should be provided by the courts or whether they should await action from Parliament.[4] That debate, however important, is not one that I wish to enter into here.

Instead, I would like to consider whether privacy is recognised as a human right in English *public* law. At the international level, the right to privacy has been recognised in the post-war international Bill of Rights,[5] although it was

---

[1] This essay is based on a talk which was given at the Administrative Law Bar Association's conference on Judicial Review and Human Rights at Cambridge on 6 July 1996.

[2] See P Atiyah, *Pragmatism and Theory in English Law* (London, Stevens, 1987) at 18–26 and 112–25.

[3] It is noteworthy that all of these of causes of action, at least in origin, are proprietary in character. Recent case-law such as *Hellewell* v. *Chief Constable of Derbyshire* [1995] 1 WLR 804 (which I look at *infra*) has started to move the law of breach of confidence away from rights of property and towards recognition of what Laws J there said might be called a right to privacy.

[4] See, for example, Lord Bingham of Cornhill CJ, "Should there be a Law to Protect Rights of Personal Privacy?" [1996] EHRLR 450; D Eady QC, "A Statutory Right to Privacy" [1996] EHRLR 243; A Lester QC, "English Judges as Law Makers" [1993] PL 269 at 284–6.

[5] Article 17 of the International Covenant on Civil and Political Rights provides: "(1) No one shall be subjected to arbitrary or unlawful interference with his privacy, family, home or correspondence, nor to unlawful attacks on his honour and reputation. (2) Everyone has the right to the protection of the law against such interference or attacks." This is almost identical to the wording of Article 12 of the Universal Declaration of Human Rights. Article 8 of the European Convention on Human Rights provides: "(1) Everyone has the right to respect for his private and family life, his home and correspondence. (2) There shall be no interference by a public authority with the exercise of this right except such as is in accordance with the law and is necessary in a democratic society in the interests of national security, public safety or the economic well-being of the country, for the prevention of disorder or crime, or for the protection of health and morals."

not expressly to be found in early bills of rights.[6] The notion of fundamental rights in public law is a novel and developing one, as I have suggested in Chapter 1. Such rights are not rights as they would be understood in a private law sense: they do not give rise to a cause of action as such. However, they may properly be understood as a zone of protection thrown around an individual which the state may not enter unless it is necessary to do so for some countervailing public interest. In that sense, since public law is concerned with the actions of public bodies which have an impact on the interests of individuals, privacy could well be regarded as an interest which is of fundamental value to English public law. A decision which intrudes on that zone of protection may attract the attention of *public* law: as I have suggested in Chapter 1, public law may require procedural fairness before the decision is taken and may even scrutinise the substance of the decision to assess its rationality in a more rigorous fashion than it would if no human right were at stake.

There is another problem about the right to privacy, which is not confined to English law. It is a question of definition but is more than a linguistic problem. It has enormous practical consequences. In the USA, for example, it has been the source of one of the most bitter controversies which divide the electorate: the question of whether the US Constitution protects a woman's right to choose to have an abortion and, if so, to what extent that right may be regulated by the state.[7] Again, I do not want here to become embroiled in the debate about the scope of the right to privacy, save to the extent that I will suggest that the recognition which has been given to privacy as an interest worthy of protection by public law embraces a wider notion than the traditional, or narrow, concept of "control over personal information".[8]

I would, however, like to look briefly at two aspects of the right to privacy as it has been understood in various jurisdictions around the world. The first

[6] For example, the US Constitution itself contains no express reference to privacy but does protect at least elements of the interest in privacy through, for example, the prohibition of unreasonable searches and seizures in the Fourth Amendment. The "constitutional" right to privacy was articulated in the case-law of the US Supreme Court in cases such as *Griswold* v. *Connecticutt* 381 US 479 (1965), where it was held that the state could not prevent married couples from using contraceptives.

[7] See e.g. *Roe* v. *Wade* 410 US 113 (1973); *Webster* v. *Reproductive Health Services* 492 US 490 (1989).

[8] For an example of the traditional view see R Wacks, "The Poverty of 'Privacy'" (1980) 96 LQR 73 especially at 77–8: "The 'right to privacy' has come a long way since its original formulation as a protection against gossip. It has grown so large that it now threatens to devour itself. Denying an individual an abortion or long hair, or subjecting him to advertising or surveillance are merely some of the activities which the American law happily accommodates under the wing of 'privacy'." For an example of the broader view of privacy see D Feldman, "Secrecy, Dignity, or Autonomy? Views of Privacy as a Civil Liberty" (1994) 47 CLP (Part 2) 41 especially at 55: "An assertion of privacy entails a moral claim that, within the circle in question, one is *prima facie* entitled to be free of outside coercion in the choice of values and standards, and to have that freedom protected by law, while recognizing that these entitlements are subject to the right of the wider society to protect the interests of vulnerable individuals within the circle and the interests of society as a whole outside it. The core of privacy as a civil liberty, then, is this entitlement to dignity and autonomy within a social circle. Secrecy, the control over information, serves, but does not exhaust that entitlement."

is to do with control over personal information, which (as I have suggested) is the traditional view of what privacy means. The information will often be contained in paper documents but in the modern world may be found in electronic data, in a photograph or in an audio or video recording. In jurisdictions such as many of the states of the United States, personal information tends to be protected by the law of tort and may give rise to an action in private law so that damages and an injunction may be obtained for infringement of privacy. But the second aspect of privacy is just as important and might be called the "constitutional" right to privacy, by which I mean that there is a zone of private decision-making and action available to the individual, into which it is not normally permissible for the coercive power of the state to intrude. The constitutional right to privacy has a particularly important – though controversial – aspect, which concerns sexual identity and intimacy.

As I have suggested earlier in this book, it may be that practitioners who are interested in developing the protection of human rights in English law and procedure need to go back to hidden seams in the common law, avenues which may have been, if not closed for many decades or centuries, ignored and neglected. We are increasingly told by the courts that privacy is a value recognised by the English common law, most recently in *R* v. *Khan (Sultan)*. To quote just one passage from the speech of Lord Nicholls of Birkenhead:

> ". . . the appellant contended for a right to privacy in respect of private conversations in private houses. I prefer to express no view, either way, on the existence of such a right. This right, if it exists, can only do so as part of a larger and wider right of privacy. The difficulties attendant on this controversial subject are well-known. Equally well-known is the continuing, widespread concern at the apparent failure of the law to give individuals a reasonable degree of protection from unwarranted intrusion in many situations. I prefer to leave open for another occasion the important question whether the present, piecemeal protection of privacy has now developed to the extent that a more comprehensive principle can be seen to exist."[9]

My suggestion to practitioners in the field would be that if we are seriously interested in helping the courts to devise comprehensive principles for the protection of privacy, at the very least we need to be aware of what is the piecemeal protection of privacy currently provided by English law.

And that may require us to reopen our history books and perhaps to go back to cases that are either ignored or regarded as trite today. An American book by Ernst and Schwarz[10] traces the right to privacy in English cases going back at least to 1741, although the authors recognise that for a long time, English law tended to protect property, not privacy as such.

As I said in Chapter 1, although not everyone would agree with me, *Entick* v. *Carrington* provides in all but name a recognition of privacy as a value in

---

[9] [1996] 3 WLR 162 at 176.

[10] M L Ernst & A U Schwartz, *Privacy: The Right to be Let Alone* (London, MacGibbon and Kee, 1968) at 5–9.

the common law. References to that value are to be found in the law reports throughout the centuries.

One recent example arises in the field of the powers of the Inland Revenue to acquire information not only from the taxpayer but also from third parties such as banks. Few of us are aware that information concerning our bank accounts can be compulsorily sought pursuant to powers in the Taxes Management Act 1970.[11] But the approach that the courts have consistently adopted in supervising the exercise of that power is to recognise that it is an intrusion on privacy and to scrutinise the apparently wide power with care.[12]

One particular issue relating to privacy that arises in practice concerns the following sort of situation. Take the powers of public bodies such as the Inland Revenue or local authorities to acquire information compulsorily. If we reflect for a moment it is obvious that such powers are necessary in a modern society in the interest of all of us. Otherwise, the fraudulent tax evader or the drug smuggler could not be properly investigated. Is there any control over the use that may then be made of the information so acquired? There are hints that the courts are prepared to develop the law, combining principles of administrative law with principles of equity, in particular the equitable action for breach of confidence, so as to generate a more general protection for people against the misuse of information which has been acquired compulsorily.[13] The argument might run in this way.

Lawyers are familiar with the fundamental doctrine of public law that powers are conferred on public bodies for certain purposes only and that the powers must be exercised so as to promote and not impede or frustrate the policy and objectives of the statute which confers the power.[14] It could readily be argued therefore that if a power has been conferred by a statute for a particular purpose, for example the investigation of tax fraud, it may not be passed on willy nilly to other public bodies for *other* purposes (however understandable) and certainly not to the media for the purpose of making profit or perhaps for the purpose of titillating members of the public. Some support for that kind of argument is provided by the important case of *Marcel* v. *Commissioner of Police for the Metropolis*.[15] There, at first instance, Sir Nicolas Browne-Wilkinson V-C said:

> "Search and seizure under statutory powers constitute fundamental infringements of the individual's immunity from interference by the state with his property and privacy – fundamental human rights . . . In my judgment, subject to any express

---

[11] Sections 20ff.

[12] See e.g. *R* v. *IRC, ex p. T C Coombs & Co* [1991] 2 AC 283; *R* v. *O'Kane and Clarke, ex p. Northern Bank Ltd* [1996] STC 1249.

[13] This would not be the first time that doctrines of public law have been influenced by the principles of private law. For example, the concept of legitimate expectation owes much to the requirements of estoppel in private law: see *R* v. *Inland Revenue Commissioners, ex p. MFK Underwriting Agents Ltd* [1990] 1 WLR 1545 at 1569H–1570B (Bingham LJ).

[14] See *Padfield* v. *Minister of Agriculture* [1968] AC 997 at 1030 (Lord Reid).

[15] [1992] Ch 225.

statutory provision in other Acts, the police are authorised to seize, retain and use documents only for public purposes related to the investigation and prosecution of crime and the return of stolen property to the true owner . . . It may also be, though I do not decide, that there are other public authorities to which the documents can properly be disclosed, for example to City or other regulatory authorities or to the security services. But in my judgment the powers to seize and retain are conferred for the better performance of *public* functions by *public bodies* and cannot be used to make information available to *private* individuals for their *private* purposes."[16]

In the Court of Appeal, although the order of the Vice-Chancellor was varied, the judgments of the Court do not suggest that it differed from him on the relevant principles. Nolan LJ said:

"The statutory powers given to the police are plainly coupled with a public law duty. The precise extent of the duty is, I think, difficult to define in general terms beyond saying that the powers must only be exercised in the public interest and with due regard to the rights of individuals. In the context of seizure and retention of documents, I would hold that the public law duty is combined with a private law duty of confidentiality towards the owner of the documents. The private law duty . . . arises from the relationship between the parties. It matters not, to my mind, that in this instance, so far as the owners of the documents are concerned, the confidence is unwillingly imparted."[17]

Sir Christopher Slade said:

"In my judgment, documents seized by a public authority from a private citizen in the exercise of a statutory power can properly be used only for those purposes for which the relevant legislation contemplated that they might be used. The user for any other purpose of documents seized in exercise of a draconian power of this nature, without the consent of the person from whom they were seized, would be an improper exercise of the power. Any such person would be entitled to expect that the authority would treat the documents and their contents as confidential, save to the extent that it might use them for purposes contemplated by the relevant legislation."[18]

This is a theme to which Robert Walker J returned recently in *Soden* v. *Burns* in which he said:

"When an official or an official body of any sort obtains information under compulsory powers for public purposes, a qualified obligation of confidence arises, though it may be overridden where transmission of confidential information is required in the public interest."[19]

I would like to touch briefly on one other issue that I know concerns human rights organisations such as Liberty in the context of the use of personal information by public authorities. This is the question of surveillance – both by

---

[16] *Ibid.* at 234D and 235C–D (*original emphasis*).
[17] *Ibid.* at 261A–B.
[18] *Ibid.* at 262C–D.
[19] [1996] 3 All ER 967 at 977d.

photographic means (in particular through the ubiquitous video camera) and by the recording of private conversations. We shall not necessarily get much comfort from the institutions in Strasbourg if we want to refine protection for privacy in this kind of area. I am sorry to say that so far the organs there view the right as being confined to private places.[20] In my view that is a distorted and out-of-date view to take.

We shall get more assistance if we look to other jurisdictions. One with which I am familiar is the United States. There in *Katz* v. *United States*[21] the US Supreme Court rejected the argument (which had earlier found favour in its case-law) that police eavesdropping by way of a "tap" on a public telephone box was lawful because such a public place is not a constitutionally protected area. The Court stressed that what the Constitution protects is people, not places. It developed the principle as this: people have a reasonable expectation that their private conversations – or perhaps (I would suggest) merely the fact of their presence in a certain place in a public place – are entitled to protection even though it might be said on one view that if they do something or say something in public they forfeit the shield of privacy.

A similar view to mine is taken by Professor Feldman, who suggests that the accumulation of information on video tapes will violate Article 8 of the ECHR if carried on without legal checks and safeguards:

> "Where closed-circuit television or similar techniques are used by the police or security services, as organs of the state, there is no legal regulation of the storage of the fruits of surveillance such as might meet these requirements . . . There seems, therefore, to be a major gap in the way in which the right to respect for private and family life is secured in the United Kingdom."[22]

If I am right that people can have a reasonable expectation of privacy in what they say or do in public places then it would be arguable that the developing law of breach of confidence should impress a stamp of confidentiality on, for example, the video tapes which are produced by surveillance cameras and on the tape recordings made by long-range microphones that can catch conversations without people even being aware that they are being listened to. Whether the remedy for such interference should be an equitable action in private law for breach of confidence or an application for judicial review in public law is a difficult question which will have to be worked out in the case-

---

[20] See S H Naismith, "Photographs, Privacy and Freedom of Expression" [1996] EHRLR 150 at 151–4.

[21] 389 US 347 (1967), especially the concurring Opinion of Justice Harlan at 516.

[22] D Feldman, "Privacy-related Rights and their Social Value" in P. Birks (ed.) *Privacy and Loyalty* (Oxford, OUP, 1997) 15–50. See also D Feldman, "Secrecy, Dignity or Autonomy? Views of Privacy as a Civil Liberty" (1994) 47 CLP (Part 2) 41 at 59–62, especially at 61 where Professor Feldman says: "A person who loses some part of the right to privacy, such as the right to be free from surveillance, when in public, may retain other privacy-related rights, such as a right to control the unauthorized or illicit use of the information gleaned from that surveillance. Privacy involves a bundle of interests, rather than a single right, so loss of part of the bundle does not entail loss of the whole."

law but the limited authorities to date suggest that either may be available in the right sort of case.[23] Again I am comforted to know that Professor Feldman takes the view that such cases could be brought by way of judicial review:

"Cases concerning the power of the police to retain or apply material seized or created in a criminal investigation for purposes tangential to that investigation could be litigated by way of judicial review, but in practice *Marcel v. Commissioner of Police for the Metropolis* and *Hellewell v. Chief Constable of Derbyshire* took the form of private law claims which Browne-Wilkinson V-C and the Court of Appeal in the former case, and Laws J in the latter, resolved into a kind of extension of the doctrine of confidentiality."[24]

The reference to *Hellewell* is to an important case in which Laws J held that photographs (commonly called "mugshots") taken compulsorily by the police are subject to the law of confidence and may not be disclosed unless it is in the public interest to do so, an obvious example of such public interest consisting in the prevention of crime. Laws J went on to say in important *obiter dicta* that:

"If someone with a telephoto lens were to take from a distance and with no authority a picture of another engaged in some private act, his subsequent disclosure of the photograph would, in my judgment, as surely amount to a breach of confidence as if he had found or stolen a letter or diary in which the act was recounted and proceeded to publish it."[25]

To conclude on this kind of privacy, there is plenty of scope for argument that a public authority has exceeded or abused its powers if it acquires confidential information for one purpose and then discloses it for another. To quote from the resounding judgment of Sir Nicolas Browne-Wilkinson V-C in *Marcel*:

"If the information obtained by the police, the Inland Revenue, the social security offices, the health service and other agencies were to be gathered together in one file, the freedom of the individual would be gravely at risk. The dossier of private information is the badge of the totalitarian state."[26]

I should move to the other aspect of privacy which I outlined earlier: the constitutional right to privacy or what I have called a zone of private decision-making in intimate areas of a person's life. This has particular impor-

---

[23] See *Hellewell* v. *Chief Constable of Derbyshire* [1995] 1 WLR 804 (Laws J), a private law action discussed in R Singh, "Privacy and the Unauthorised Publication of Photographs" (1995) 139 SJ 771; R v. *Brentwood BC, ex p. Peck* (unreported, 18 October 1996) in which leave to move for judicial review was granted by Hidden J after an oral hearing, leave having been refused on the papers by Buxton J. In *Marcel, supra,* n. 15 in particular at 261A–B, Nolan LJ suggested that what is in play where confidential information is acquired by compulsion is both a public law duty and a private law duty.

[24] D Feldman, 'To What Extent Can Public Law Protect the Right to Respect for Private Life?' (Unpublished paper given to the Administrative Law Bar Association on 6 July 1996) at pp.14–15.

[25] *supra* n. 23 at 807G–H.

[26] *Supra* n.15 at 240C–D.

tance in the field of sexual intimacy and the power of individuals in a free society to choose their sexual identity and orientation and to choose with whom they will develop sexual relationships. This is something that I am happy to say has been better developed by the Strasbourg institutions than across the Atlantic in the USA.[27] The Strasbourg institutions are usually receptive to arguments based on US case-law, for example in the field of abortion rights.[28] On the other hand the US Supreme Court has largely ignored what the Strasbourg institutions have had to say on issues similar to the one they have had to decide, most notoriously in the field of gay rights, perhaps because the cases were not cited to them. In a powerful dissent in the leading case of *Bowers* v. *Hardwick* Justice Blackmun, with whom three other members of the Supreme Court agreed, defined the constitutional right to privacy as well as anyone can:

> "'Our cases long have recognised that the Constitution embodies a promise that a certain sphere of individual liberty will be kept largely beyond the reach of government.' In construing the right to privacy, the Court has proceeded along two, somewhat distinct, albeit complementary, lines. First, it has recognised a privacy interest with reference to certain *decisions* that are properly for the individual to make. Second, it has recognised a privacy interest with reference to certain *places* without regard for the particular activities in which the individuals who occupy them are engaged. The case before us implicates both the decisional and the spatial aspects of the right to privacy . . .

> Only the most willful blindness could obscure the fact that sexual intimacy is 'a sensitive, key relationship of human existence, central to family life, community welfare, and the development of human personality' . . . The fact that individuals define themselves in a significant way through their intimate sexual relationships with others suggests, in a Nation as diverse as ours, that there may be many 'right' ways of conducting those relationships, and that much of the richness of a relationship will come from the freedom an individual has to *choose* the form and nature of these intensely personal bonds."[29]

Bowers itself concerned a statute that it may be surprising to learn still exists in about half of the states of America: a statute which criminalises even consenting acts of homosexuality between adults in private. The message from the dissenting Opinion of Justice Blackmun is clear: these matters are not usually the business of the court or of government.

I would suggest that this second kind of privacy right, the freedom of decision making in the sexual sphere, is one that can now properly be said to be recognised by the English common law too. The *Smith*[30] case is an important case for all sorts of reasons, not least the court's acceptance of the principle that the justification for a decision affecting human rights may be reviewed

---

[27] See *Dudgeon* v. *United Kingdom* Series A, No 45 (1982) 4 EHRR 149.
[28] See *Brüggemann and Scheuten* v. *Germany* (App 6959/75) 10 DR 100 (1978).
[29] 478 US 186 (1986) at 203 to 206.
[30] *R* v. *Ministry of Defence, ex p. Smith* [1996] QB 517.

for irrationality,[31] which is the nearest concept we have to a principle of proportionality in English public law.

But what I want to focus on here is: what is the human right at stake in a case like *Smith*? Unless there is a human right at stake, why go into questions as to whether that infringement is justified? It is quite clear that the right which the Court of Appeal recognised is a right to respect for private life which includes what I have called a constitutional right to privacy, at least in sexual matters. Sir Thomas Bingham MR (as he then was) said:

> "The present cases do not concern the lives or liberty [*sc.* personal liberty] of those involved. But they do concern innate qualities of a very personal kind and the decisions of which the appellants complain have had a profound effect on their careers and prospects."[32]

Later, in the context of whether there was a violation of Article 8 of the ECHR (an issue that the Court declined to decide since it was a matter for the Strasbourg institutions), the Master of the Rolls said:

> ". . . to dismiss a person from his or her employment on the grounds of a private sexual preference, and to interrogate him or her about private sexual behaviour, would not appear to me to show respect for that person's private and family life."[33]

Smith in my view indicates a willingness on the part of English courts not only to acknowledge the place of privacy as a value in the common law but also to give it a wide scope. If one reflects on what is being said there, this is nothing to do with privacy in the traditional sense of keeping secret personal information or even about a consensual act in a private place free from observation by other people. This is a situation where somebody is declaring their sexual identity to a public body (the armed forces) saying that: "I have the right to be treated with respect for the identity which I have chosen for myself and you have no right to dismiss me from service for Queen and country because you do not like it." So the common law displays its remarkable (and commendable) ability to transform itself in a generation. Acts which were until 1967 potentially criminal may now be regarded as a part of a person's private life and as such to be provided protection by public law (albeit through the inadequate doctrine of irrationality).

I would like to end by returning to the theme I started with. It falls to practitioners to find dicta here and there, points along the path, so they can suggest to the court that there is a thread of principle and then to assist the courts in performing their proper role of providing adequate protection for privacy, the "comprehensive principle" of which Lord Nicholls spoke in *Khan*. The seminal article by Warren and Brandeis[34] is often cited as the genesis of the tort of breach of privacy in American states. It is ironic that the article relied

---

[31] See *supra* p. 42.
[32] [1996] QB 517 at 556.
[33] At 558G.
[34] S D Warren & L D Brandeis, "The Right to Privacy" (1890) 4 Harvard LR 193.

upon many cases in English jurisprudence, including *Prince Albert* v. *Strange.*[35] This country has done a great deal for the protection of human rights around the world generally and to provide a right of privacy in particular. It would be fitting if it were recognised as a right in English law. Privacy, like human rights generally (if not football), may at last be coming home.

[35] 2 DeGex and Sm 652 (1849).

6

Freedom of Movement as a Human Right in English Law[1]

The importance of freedom of movement as a human right can hardly be overestimated. In our own time, tyrannical regimes have relied on controlling people's movement to prop themselves up and oppress despised minorities or even majorities. In South Africa, the notorious pass laws and the group areas legislation were essential tools for the implementation of apartheid. In the USSR, internal exile and restrictions on exit visas were the means necessary to suppress political and religious dissidents. And in places such as Albania, rigid control over who could enter the country was thought necessary in order to maintain their system of government. Although it already seems like a long time ago, it was only in 1989 that the Berlin Wall, and the fortress mentality which it violently represented, was pulled down.

On the other hand, liberal societies throughout the ages have tended to welcome strangers. For example, in his funeral oration the great Athenian democrat, Pericles, said of Athens in the fifth century BC that "our city is open to the world" and that it was the school of Greece: open borders can be the hallmark of what Sir Karl Popper called "the open society".[2] Nevertheless, the power of a state to control who may enter its territory has traditionally been regarded as an essential aspect of its sovereignty. Such control provides an important means to pursue such governmental goals as the detection of crime (particularly drugs offences), the prevention of terrorism, and (perhaps most controversially) the protection of the domestic labour market and social security systems from those who are regarded as being outsiders and therefore as not having full claims on the community's resources.

I say that this is controversial because, although it is now accepted as almost self-evident that so-called "economic migrants" should not be received into Western Europe, freedom of movement has historically been valued precisely because it gave people the chance to change their lives for the better by looking for jobs and homes. This is how countries such as the United States

---

[1] This essay is based on a seminar given at Queen Mary and Westfield College, London on 20 November 1996, which was chaired by His Honour Judge David Pearl, the Chief Immigration Adjudicator.

[2] Thucydides, *The Peloponnesian War* (tr R Warner) (Harmondsworth, Penguin, 1972), at 146; K Popper, *The Open Society and Its Enemies* (Golden Jubilee edn) (London, Routledge, 1995) at 186–7.

became what they are today and indeed what lies behind the free movement rights in European Community law – about which I shall say more later.

The law of the United Kingdom has in the postwar era gone through a difficult transition from Empire to Commonwealth to membership of what we now call the European Union. It has gone from a relatively open system of entry for those who were citizens of a Commonwealth country to a system where "patriality" (later British citizenship[3]) became crucial to a position where nationality of one of the Member States of the EU has arguably become the most significant status, since such nationality gives access to the free movement rights in Articles 48, 52 and 59 of the EC Treaty and to the important but still unclear concept of citizenship of the European Union conferred by Article 8 of that Treaty as amended by the Maastricht Treaty (the Treaty on European Union).[4]

Perhaps surprisingly, the constitutions of modern liberal states did not until relatively recently include provisions as to freedom of movement – at least for people, as opposed to commerce. For example, the US Constitution expressly provided for freedom of interstate commerce but had no express provision on free movement by people. Nevertheless the jurisprudence of the courts has filled this gap and recognised freedom of movement as a fundamental right: see *Aptheker* v. *Secretary of State*[5] in which the US Supreme Court held that freedom to travel abroad was one of the privileges of US citizenship[6] and, in the process, helped to dismantle one of the vestiges of the Macarthy era, the denial of passports to members of the Communist Party under the Internal Security Act of 1950. In an important case called *Shapiro* v. *Thompson*[7] the Supreme Court held that a statute which distinghished between two classes of residents, those who had resided in the State for at least a year and therefore qualified for welfare assistance and those who had been resident for less than a year and therefore did not qualify for such assistance, violated a person's constitutional right to free movement as between States. In passing, the case can also be regarded as an example of where a court, in enforcing a tradi-

---

[3] It is only British citizens, strictly so called, who have the right of abode in the United Kingdom: see section 1 of the Immigration Act 1971, as amended by the British Nationality Act 1981. It is arguable that other types of citizenship created by the 1981 Act, though not conferring the right of abode, make a person a British national for the purposes of international law: see I Macdonald & N Blake, *Immigration Law and Practice* 4th edn (London, Butterworth, 1995) at 423.

[4] For a recent judicial comment stressing the practical importance of British citizenship, especially because of the access to Community law rights which it gives, see *R* v. *Secretary of State for the Home Department, ex p. Fayed* [1997] 1 All ER 228 at 237 (Lord Woolf MR).

[5] 378 US 500 (1964).

[6] Protected by Article IV, section 2 of the US Constitution; see also the Fourteenth Amendment.

[7] 394 US 618 (1969). See also *Edwards* v. *California* 314 US 160 (1941) in which the Supreme Court held that a statute prohibiting anyone from bringing a non-resident indigent person into the state violated the clause in Article I, section 8 of the US Constitution which protects the freedom of interstate commerce.

tional civil right, may indirectly give effect to social and economic rights as well – something which I have already considered in Chapter 3.

At the international level, freedom of movement is expressly protected by the International Covenant on Civil and Political Rights in Article 12 as follows:

> "(1) Everyone lawfully within the territory of a State shall, within that territory, have the right to liberty of movement and freedom to choose his residence.
>
> (2) Everyone shall be free to leave any country, including his own.
>
> . . .
>
> (4) No one shall be arbitrarily deprived of the right to enter his own country."[8]

As with so many human rights, freedom of movement has an ancient pedigree, going back to Magna Carta:

> "It shall be lawful to any person, for the future, to go out of our Kingdom, and to return, safely and securely, by land or by water, saving his allegiance to us, unless it be in time of war, for some short space, for the common good of the Kingdom . . ."[9]

Incidentally, that proviso could be regarded as an early use of the concept of proportionality in our law – and in the context of what would today be called "national security".

In English law, freedom of movement has been protected through the traditional method of the common law: whatever is not prohibited by some rule of law to an individual is permitted, and this includes movement. The main inhibition would be the rights of others, including in particular the right to private property: clearly, your right to move is limited by who owns the land on which you wish to travel. The main mechanism through which it is protected by the common law is through the torts of false imprisonment and other forms of trespass to the person.

However, as with other human rights, it has become apparent that adequate protection for freedom of movement requires that there should be positive protection for the right against the actions of government – even if there is apparent legal authority for such action. The main source of this positive right within domestic law has been European Community ("EC") law.

EC law, at least in origin, was primarily concerned with economic rights rather than human rights. Moreover, EC law is usually concerned with the relationship between the national of one Member State and the authorities of another Member State. Human rights, in contrast, are usually concerned with the relationship between a national and his or her own state and/or with the

---

[8] The United Kingdom has made a general reservation covering immigration and nationality when it reports to the UN Human Rights Committee, which supervises implementation of the International Covenant, although doubt has been expressed as to the validity of that reservation: see Macdonald & Blake *supra* n.3 at 422. See further, on relevant international and comparative materials, P Sieghart, *The International Law of Human Rights* (Oxford, OUP, 1983) at 174–88.

[9] Ch. 42 in the version confirmed by Edward I in 1297: *Halsbury's Statutes* Vol 10, at 17.

relationship between everyone, irrespective of nationality, and a state. What I would like to explore is the extent to which EC law can be used to reach beyond its traditional concern to deal with these two additional situations. As Gráinne de Búrca has put it: "individual freedom of movement within the Community has more than a commercial value."[10]

Moreover, as its impact has been felt, it has become clear that the Community legal order's own lexicon of fundamental freedoms, including free movement of goods and the freedom to provide services, can be the indirect source of protection for an overlapping array of human rights, such as freedom of expression. In this chapter I would like to explore the way in which the impact of EC law may be felt in four distinct areas, and how thereby human rights may be made more effective in domestic law. Those areas are, first, freedom to cross the international borders of the United Kingdom; secondly, reverse discrimination under EC law, that is, situations where it is alleged that a UK national is treated less favourably than nationals of other Member States of the European Union; thirdly, freedom to move around within the United Kingdom, for example between Northern Ireland and Great Britain; and, fourthly, the indirect protection of other human rights through the free movement rights conferred by EC law, for example the protection of freedom of expression by use of Article 30 of the EC Treaty.

But before I consider each of those in more detail, I should make some general observations about the relationship between EC law and domestic law, especially so far as it may be a vehicle for the indirect absorption of human rights principles by domestic law.

It is a truism that EC law is capable of having direct effect: it may confer rights on individuals which may be asserted in, and must be protected by, national courts and tribunals.[11] It is also well-known that such rights are superior to rules of domestic law, which must give way to them in case of conflict.[12]

Respect for human rights is one of the general principles of EC law: see *Nold* v. *Commission*[13] where the European Court of Justice ("ECJ") accepted that:

"International treaties for the protection of human rights on which the Member States have collaborated or of which they are signatories, can supply guidelines which should be followed within the framework of EC law."

One of the sources of such human rights law to which the ECJ will look is the European Convention on Human Rights ("ECHR"). This is so not only where an act of an institution of the European Union is challenged but even

[10] G. de Búrca, "Fundamental Human Rights and the Reach of EC Law" (1993) 13 OJLS 283 at 299.
[11] Case 26/62 *Van Gend en Loos* v. *Nederlandse Administratie der Belastingen* [1963] ECR 1; Case 41/74 *Van Duyn* v. *Home Office* [1974] ECR 1337.
[12] Case 6/64 *Costa* v. *ENEL* [1964] ECR 585.
[13] Case 4/73 [1974] ECR 507.

where it is the act of a Member State which is under scrutiny: see for example *Johnston* v. *Chief Constable of the RUC*,[14] where the ECJ looked at Article 6 of the ECHR (the right to a fair hearing by a court in the determination of civil rights) in the context of the national authorities' derogation from the principle of equal treatment for men and women.

As Lord Browne-Wilkinson put it in his 1991 Harry Street Lecture:

"Although in *Brind v. Secretary of State for the Home Department* the House of Lords refused to give effect to the ECHR 'by the back door' so long as Parliament by failing to incorporate it had not admitted it by the front door, in one area Parliament has left the back door open. In that area we already enjoy a full Bill of Rights: the Convention is directly enforceable in our courts."[15]

The only reservation I have is with the use of the word "directly". I would prefer to say that an act of a Member State that derogates from a Community law right may be assessed not only directly in accordance with EC law but indirectly against the law of the ECHR. This would presumably be so even though the particular Member State of the European Union has not ratified the part of the ECHR being relied upon. As is well-known, the United Kingdom has not ratified the Fourth Protocol to the ECHR, Article 3(2) of which provides that: "No one shall be deprived of the right to enter the territory of the State of which he is a national." But, if someone could identify a EC law right which they can assert against the United Kingdom, then that provision could become relevant anyway.[16]

So far as domestic law itself is concerned, freedom of movement has been recognised as a human right in the common law, which marches in step with ECHR and EC law in this, and other, contexts today: see *R* v. *Secretary of State for the Home Department, ex p. McQuillan*,[17] where Sedley J said that "freedom of movement, subject only to the general law, is a fundamental value of the common law." The practical significance of this, leaving aside the intervention of EC law, has yet to be worked out by UK courts.

Turning then to EC law itself, it is well-known that free movement of persons is one of the fundamental freedoms of the EC legal order, along with free movement of goods, services and capital. It is governed by Article 48 (which confers the right of free movement for workers),[18] Article 52 (which confers

---

[14] Case 222/84 [1986] ECR 1651.

[15] Lord Browne-Wilkinson, "The Infiltration of a Bill of Rights" [1992] PL 397 at 401. See also N Grief, "The Domestic Impact of the European Convention on Human Rights as Mediated through Community Law" [1991] PL 555.

[16] See further Case C–168/91 *Konstandinis* v. *Stadt Altensteig* [1993] ECR I–1191, where Advocate-General Jacobs suggested that an EU national has the right to be treated in accordance with a common code of fundamental values, including the Convention, when in the territory of another Member State: para. 46 of his Opinion.

[17] [1995] 4 All ER 400 (Sedley J) at 421j and 422h.

[18] Article 48 EC, so far as material, provides:

"1. Freedom of movement for workers shall be secured within the Community by the end of the transitional period at the latest.   *cont/*

the right to freedom of establishment) and Article 59 (which confers the right to freedom to provide services and has been held to include the freedom to receive services, for example by going abroad as a tourist[19]). Finally, under EC legislation made pursuant to those treaty provisions,[20] rights are conferred on the families of those who enjoy the right to free movement of workers, and procedures are prescribed to safeguard the rights otherwise conferred.

The first type of case I want to look at is where a person crosses the international borders of the United Kingdom. Most people – those who are not British citizens – need leave to enter the United Kingdom under the Immigration Act 1971. Classically, a person who is a national of a non-European country will need leave.[21] This is so even if they are married to a British citizen, indeed they may have to satisfy certain requirements which apply to married couples such as the primary purpose rule (that is prove that it was not their primary purpose in contracting the marriage to enter the UK).[22] Does EC law alter any of this? The answer is that it may do so, provided the situation is not what the ECJ calls "wholly internal".

The provisions of the EC Treaty on free movement are not normally concerned with the relationship between a Member State and one of its own nationals, at least so far as activities on its own territory are concerned. This is because it is a wholly internal situation.[23] Moreover, it will not avail someone to complain that they are treated less favourably than another Member State's nationals are treated by that other state. EC law does not require state A to treat its own nationals no less favourably than *state B* treats its own nationals.[24]

However, if it can be shown that the same state (let us take the United Kingdom as an example) discriminates as between nationals of different

2. Such freedom of movement shall entail the abolition of any discrimination based on nationality between workers of the Member States as regards employment, remuneration and other conditions of work and employment.
3. It shall entail the right, subject to limitations justified on grounds of public policy, public security or public health:
(a) to accept offers of employment actually made;
(b) to move freely within the territory of Member States for this purpose;
(c) to stay in a Member State for the purpose of employment in accordance with the provisions governing the employment of nationals of the State laid down by law, regulation or administrative action;
(d) to remain in the territory of a Member State after having been employed in that State . . ."

[19] Cases 286/82 and 26/83 *Luisi and Carbone* v. *Ministero del Tesoro* [1984] ECR 377; Case 186/87 *Cowan* v. *Trésor Public* [1989] ECR 195.

[20] In particular Regulation 1612/68 and Directive 68/360.

[21] For those who do not need leave because they have an enforceable Community law right, see section 7(1) of the Immigration Act 1988, which was brought into force on 20 July 1994 by SI 1994/1923.

[22] HC 395, para. 281. The new Labour Government elected in May 1997 abolished the primary purposes rule in June 1997.

[23] See, for example, Cases 35 and 36/82 *Morson and Jhanjan* v. *The Netherlands* [1982] ECR 3723 especially at 3735–6, paras 12–17.

[24] Case 44/84 *Hurd* v. *Jones* [1986] ECR 29, especially at 84–5, paras 50–6; and Case 115/78 *Knoors* v. *Secretary of State for Economic Affairs* [1979] ECR 399 especially at 410, paras 24–5.

Member States, it may be possible for a British citizen to rely on EC law even against the United Kingdom. An example is provided by *R v. Immigration Appeal Tribunal, ex p. Secretary of State for the Home Department*,[25] which was concerned with the situation where state A gives fewer rights as to residence to a returning national of state A (to be accompanied by his or her spouse) than it gives to a national of state B.[26] Moreover, that case shows how even third-country nationals may indirectly enjoy the benefit of EC law in limited circumstances: there Mr Singh, a national of India, was able to enjoy rights under EC law against the United Kingdom by virtue of his marriage to a British citizen. Furthermore, it showed that the fact of movement across an interstate frontier within the EU may trigger more favourable rights for a British citizen against the UK Government than would be available to other British citizens against their own government. That can be the remarkable effect of the "magic wand" of EC law.

This brings me to my second type of situation: the concept of reverse discrimination. What if there is no actual movement across a frontier within the EU? In principle, this should not matter, since any impediment to freedom of movement, including *outward* movement, should *prima facie* be a breach of Article 48. An example would be the restriction on transfer of footballers considered in *Bosman*,[27] where the ECJ said:

> "Provisions which preclude or deter a national of a Member State from leaving his country of origin in order to exercise his right to freedom of movement . . . constitute an obstacle to that freedom even if they apply without regard to the nationality of the workers concerned . . ."

Although the subject is not free from doubt, it seems that the logic of *Bosman* would apply to a footballer in his own country who has never moved as well as to the many foreign players now in the United Kingdom. On the other hand, is the mere fact of movement sufficient to trigger EC law? Clearly if I go to Calais on a "booze cruise" (not that I would) and come back after a day, it does not follow that I can start complaining about acts of the United Kingdom which have nothing to do with that trip but which I say are in breach of EC law. Sometimes the attempt to use EC law against one's own state can be taken too far.

Perhaps I could illustrate this with a case decided by the Employment Appeal Tribunal ("EAT") *Birchall v. Secretary of State for Education*.[28] The appellant was at one time employed by a local education authority and, had he chosen to remain in their employment, would have been required to retire at the age of sixty-five. He obtained employment by the Secretary of State at

---

[25] Case C–370/90: this case is often referred to as *Surinder Singh* [1992] ECR I–4265.

[26] *Ibid.* at paras 15–23.

[27] Case C–415/93 *Union Royale Belge des Sociétés de Football Association v. Bosman* [1995] ECR I–4921, para 96.

[28] Unreported, 20 September 1996 (EAT). I appeared as junior counsel for the Secretary of State in this case.

the European School, which has a number of establishments around the European Union and provides education for the children of European civil servants: one of the schools is in Culham, near Oxford. In the United Kingdom (unlike in certain other European countries) teachers are employed by local education authorities (LEAs), not by the central government. Hence it is necessary for the government unusually to employ teachers directly in order to fulfil its obligations under the Statute of the European School. The appellant now had a retirement age of sixty, in line with ordinary civil service rules.

The appellant had actually moved in the course of his work, from the LEA to Brussels and back to Culham. Other teachers at the European School working at Culham were employed by their own states, in accordance with their own national rules: for example, their retirement age might well be sixty-five or even higher. The appellant argued that Article 48 had been infringed here either:

(1) because he was discriminated against (directly or indirectly) on the ground of his nationality; or
(2) because dismissal in the circumstances of his case impeded the free movement of workers even in the absence of discrimination.

The EAT accepted the argument on behalf of the respondent that a person cannot rely on the mere fact of movement across one of the frontiers between Member States unless they can also show a causal nexus between the denial of the right or benefit in question and the right of free movement. This is supported by the Opinion of the Advocate-General in *Surinder Singh*,[29] namely that the denial of the right or benefit is objectionable only in so far as it is an impediment to the right of free movement, and is not an independent source of objection.

The appellant's legal position was no different because he went to the European School in Brussels and then returned than it would have been if he had gone at the outset to Brussels or to Culham and stayed there throughout the remainder of his teaching career. Contrast the British national in *Surinder Singh* who had greater rights in Germany (to be accompanied by her spouse) than she would have on her return to the United Kingdom.

My third type of case is where it has been argued that EC law gives a person the right of free movement *within* the territory of the United Kingdom. Traditionally this argument has foundered on the doctrine that EC law is not concerned with wholly internal situations. So, in *R v. Saunders*[30] the ECJ held that a form of internal exile, which was effected by attaching a condition to a binding-over order, was not covered by the free movement rights in the EC Treaty. Similarly, in *Moser v. Land Baden-Württemberg*[31] the ECJ held that the bar on people who have been members of the Communist Party from

---

[29] At para. 5.
[30] Case 175/78 [1979] ECR 1129.
[31] Case 180/83 [1984] ECR 2539.

becoming teachers in Germany was not covered either. That decision can be contrasted with the recent judgment of the European Court of Human Rights in *Vogt* v. *Germany*,[32] which held that dismissal (and I should emphasise that it was a dismissal case) of a teacher on that ground was excessive and not necessary in a democratic society.

It has been suggested that things may have changed as a result of Articles 8 and 8a of the EC Treaty, as amended by the Maastricht Treaty. Article 8 provides:

> "1 Citizenship of the European Union is hereby established. Every person holding the nationality of a Member State shall be a citizen of the Union . . ."

Article 8a, as inserted by the Maastricht Treaty, provides:

> "1 Every citizen of the Union shall have the right to move and reside freely within the territory of the Member States, subject to the limitations and conditions laid down in this Treaty and by the measures adopted to give it effect . . ."

At first sight it is at least arguable that the language of Article 8a, especially having regard to its purpose, does apply to what were previously called wholly internal situations, because it refers to movement "within the territory of the Member States". In *R* v. *Secretary of State for the Home Department, ex p. Adams*[33] Steyn LJ thought that the point was "seriously arguable". The applicant was the subject of an exclusion order under the Prevention of Terrorism (Temporary Provisions) Act 1989. He was – and is – the leader of Sinn Fein and had been invited to address a meeting at the House of Commons. He was banned from coming to mainland Britain. He argued that the ban violated his right to free movement under Article 8a. The Divisional Court decided to refer various questions of EC law to the ECJ, in particular on the requirements of proportionality in a case where both freedom of expression and national security were at stake. However, the reference was withdrawn after the exclusion order was lifted in the light of the IRA ceasefire in August 1994. The only case, as we shall see, in which the ECJ would have had the opportunity directly to consider the effect and scope of Article 8a was therefore removed from its jurisdiction.

Next came the decision of Sedley J in *R* v. *Secretary of State for the Home Department, ex p. McQuillan*.[34] This applicant was also the subject of an exclusion order banning him from Great Britain. He too argued that his rights under Article 8a had been violated. The High Court decided to stay further consideration of the case pending the determination of the *Adams* reference. But, even though the Adams reference was withdrawn, it seems as if Mr McQuillan has never applied to restore the case to the High Court (probably because his exclusion order was also lifted). At the end of his judgment, Sedley

---

[32] Series A, No 323 (1995) 21 EHRR 205.
[33] [1995] All ER (EC) 177 at 189a.
[34] [1995] 4 All ER 400.

J said that he was parting with the case for the time being – in fact he may be waiting some time.

In a number of cases which concerned international movement, rather than internal movement, the English courts have held that Article 8a has not had any legal effect going beyond the other provisions of the Treaty and that it does not have direct effect anyway.[35]

In *R v. Secretary of State for the Home Department, ex p. Colak*,[36] which is an early case on Article 8a, the Court of Appeal decided that, even if Article 8a did have direct effect, and even if it could be relied on by a national of a third country, it did not come into operation until there had been movement across a frontier within the EU: since the applicant had only been in the transit lounge at the airport at Paris, the first time he entered the territory of the EU was therefore when he entered the United Kingdom.

It has to be said that what the English courts have decided is "acte clair" and need not be referred to Luxembourg is something which the European Commission regards as clear the other way. Its position is both that Article 8a has changed the law, in that it has elevated freedom of movement to a constitutional status, and that it has direct effect.

Before leaving the issue of European citizenship, it is worth noting what we have created. In a slightly different context, in *Konstandinis*[37] Advocate-General Jacobs has suggested that every national of a Member State who goes to another Member State in exercise of one of the rights conferred by the EC Treaty can proclaim: "civis europeus sum" – I am a European citizen. Although it was not intended in this way, this phrase has unfortunate connotations as well. In 1850, at the time of the notorious Dom Pacifico incident, Palmerston declared that British gunboats would go around the world protecting British nationals and also compared them to Ancient Romans who could say: "civis romanus sum". In response, Gladstone made his famous speech in which he asked:

> "What then, Sir, was a Roman citizen? He was the member of a privileged caste; he belonged to a conquering race, to a nation that held all others bound down by the strong arm of power. For him there was to be an exceptional system of law; for him principles were to be asserted, and by him rights were to be enjoyed, that were denied to the rest of the world."[38]

At the end of the twentieth century, there is a danger that we are setting up an exceptional system of law where there is a privileged caste of European cit-

---

[35] See *Phull v. Secretary of State for the Home Department* [1996] Imm AR 72 at 78, where the Court of Appeal said that it would not make a reference under Article 177 of the EC Treaty because it had come to the "confident conclusion both that Article 8a is not intended to operate domestically, and also that in default of further measures it is not capable of having direct effect." See also *R v. Westminster City Council, ex p. Castelli* (1995) 28 HLR 125 (Latham J); and *R v. Secretary of State for the Home Department, ex p. Vitale* [1996] All ER (EC) 461 (CA).

[36] [1993] 3 CMLR 201 (CA).

[37] Case 168/91 [1993] ECR I–1191.

[38] R Jenkins, *Gladstone* (London, Macmillan, 1995) at 118–19.

izens, those who are nationals of Member States, while those who are nationals of third countries, and who are lawfully settled in a Member State, remain in a real sense second-class citizens.

Finally, I turn to my fourth topic: can EC law rights on free movement be used to protect human rights more generally? In my view, they can. A recent example is provided by the decision of the Court of Appeal in *R v. Human Fertilisation and Embryology Authority, ex p. Blood.*[39] The applicant was a woman whose husband had died after they had planned to have children but before she had conceived. While he was unconscious but before his death, sperm was taken from him and frozen for potential use in *in vitro* fertilisation. However, permission so to use it was refused by the respondent authority because the husband had not given his written consent and such consent was required in accordance with its rules. Both the High Court and the Court of Appeal accepted the arguments for the respondent that, under the terms of the Human Fertilisation and Embryology Act 1990, there was no breach of domestic law as such. However, the Court of Appeal decided that the respondent had erred in law because it had not taken sufficient account of the applicant's right to freedom of movement across national frontiers within the European Union in order to receive services, under Articles 59 and 60 of the EC Treaty. The Court therefore remitted the matter to the respondent for reconsideration in accordance with law. The authority on reconsideration did in fact permit the applicant to use the sperm by travelling to a clinic in Belgium where the requirement that the husband should give written consent was apparently not imposed, although the applicant would have to comply with the ethical standards laid down for the clinic there.[40]

To illustrate the potential use of EC law to promote human rights further I would like to take another example, concerning freedom of expression. The case[41] settled out of court in 1996. It concerned a ban by the Independent Television Commission on advertising by the Church of Scientology and by a publisher associated with it: the publisher was a Danish company. The ban applied even though the products that they might wish to advertise included (bestselling) works of fiction of the kind which its competitors could lawfully advertise. Moreover, the ban imposed by the ITC had very wide geographical scope: its effect was to prevent a Danish publisher from using the advertising facilities provided by (for example) a satellite and cable channel in order to advertise books in other Member States of the European Union and not only in the United Kingdom.

The applicants contended that the blanket ban challenged in this case violated Article 30 of the EC Treaty, which guarantees free movement of goods,

---

[39] [1997] 2 WLR 806.

[40] Although the case did not directly concern human rights arguments, it could be said indirectly to give effect to the right to found a family and (possibly) to the right to respect for private and family life.

[41] I was instructed as junior counsel for the applicants.

subject to the limited derogation permitted under EC law, for example on the grounds of public policy.

Article 30 applies not just to direct restrictions on imports but on all measures having "equivalent effect", for example those which have an impact upon advertising.[42]

In the classic case of *Dassonville*[43] the ECJ held that Article 30 prohibited measures which: ". . . are capable of hindering, directly or indirectly, actually or potentially, intra-EC trade". It is not necessary for a measure to discriminate between domestic goods and foreign goods for Article 30 to be relevant. In the case of "indistinctly applicable" rules, which do not discriminate in that way, the *prima facie* rule remains as asserted in the *Cassis de Dijon*[44] case:

> "Obstacles to movement within the EC resulting from disparities between the national laws relating to the marketing of products in question must be accepted *in so far as* those provisions may be recognised as being *necessary* in order to satisfy *mandatory* requirements relating in particular to the effectiveness of fiscal supervision, the protection of public health, the fairness of commercial transactions and the defence of the consumer." (*emphasis added*)

One legal issue was not resolved because the case settled. It might have been suggested that Article 30 does not apply to a case of this kind on the authority of the ECJ.[45]

However, I would suggest that the general principle remains as enunciated in *Cassis de Dijon* and that the exception to that principle in *Keck* is, on analysis, irrelevant to a case such as ours, because:

(1) *Keck* establishes that Article 30 will not apply to a measure which regulates "selling arrangements" provided it applies to all affected traders *operating within the national territory* and provided that it affects in the same manner, in law and in fact, the marketing of both domestic products and those from other Member States.[46]

(2) *TF1* applies the *Keck* doctrine to the particular context of advertising on television.[47]

(3) *Lucien* also recognises that *Keck* applies to advertising but distinguishes it on the ground that there the restriction on advertising applied only to imports and not to domestic goods, i.e. the treatment there was not neutral.[48]

---

[42] See Case 286/81 *Criminal Proceedings against Oosthoek's Uitgeversmaatschappij BV* [1982] ECR 4575 at para. 15 and Case C–362/88 *GB–INNO–BM* v. *Confédération du Commerce Luxembourgeois Asbl* [1990] ECR I–667 at para 7–8.

[43] Case 8/74 *Procureur du Roi* v. *Dassonville* [1974] ECR 837 at 852.

[44] Case 120/78 *Rewe-Zentrale AG* v. *Bundesmonopolverwaltung für Branntwein* [1979] ECR 649, especially at para 8.

[45] See Case C–267/91 *Keck and Mithouard* [1993] ECR I–6097; Case C–412/93 *Société d'Importation Edouard Leclerc-Siplec* v. *TF1 Publicité SA* [1995] ECR I–179; and Case C–320/93 *Lucien Ortschect GmbH* v. *Eurum-Pharm Arzneimittel GmbH* [1994] ECR I–5245.

[46] See para. 16 of the Judgment.

[47] See para. 21 of the Judgment.

[48] See para. 9 of the Judgment.

(4) What none of those cases dealt with was the situation where a person on whom a ban has been imposed is based in another Member State and does not operate within the national territory of (say) the United Kingdom.

(5) Even more importantly, none of those cases dealt with the situation where one Member State arrogates to itself the power to regulate advertising *elsewhere* in the European Union by reason of the fortuitous fact that a broadcaster happens to operate from the United Kingdom. The contrary conclusion would mean that UK authorities could ban an undertaking based in the Netherlands from advertising by satellite or cable in Germany, France or Italy. Such a gross interference with the integrity of the single market cannot be permissible under the EC Treaty unless it complies with the tests for mandatory requirements laid down in *Cassis de Dijon*.

(6) In any event, the reasoning of the Court in *Keck* itself has been subjected to doubt and convincing criticism, not least by Advocate-General Jacobs in *TF1*.[49]

Furthermore, any justification that might be advanced by reference to public policy would have to satisfy the test of "necessity" mentioned in *Cassis de Dijon (supra)* and accordingly would have to meet the requirement of proportionality. Finally, this question of necessity has to be considered in the light of the ECHR, as I have suggested earlier in this chapter.

The applicants' argument relied, indirectly, on Article 10 of the ECHR, which guarantees freedom of expression. Article 10 has been held to apply to commercial speech, made for the purposes of advertising.[50] Any exception made under Article 10(2) must be strictly construed.[51] Article 10 of the ECHR has been relied upon in several decisions of the ECJ. In *Oyone & Traore*,[52] the ECJ held that certain regulations:

". . . cannot be interpreted in such a way as to conflict with freedom of expression, a fundamental right which the Court must ensure is respected in EC law . . ."

In *SPUC* v. *Grogan*[53] the ECJ decided that the activities in question were not within the scope of EC law (since the student organisations there had no connection with the abortion clinics whose services they were advertising), but again indicated that EC law could not (had it applied) have been interpreted

---

[49] See paras 38–55 of his Opinion, especially at para 38.
[50] See *Casado Coca* v. *Spain* Series A, No. 285 (1994) 18 EHRR 1.
[51] See *Informationsverein Lentia* v. *Austria* Series A, No. 276 (1994) 17 EHRR 93 at 112 where the European Court of Human Rights, reiterating its conclusions in *Autronic AG* v. *Switzerland* Series A, No. 178 (1990) 12 EHRR 485 at 502–3, said that European supervision of Article 10 rights ". . . must be strict because of the importance – frequently stressed by the Court – of the rights in question. The necessity for any restriction must be convincingly established."
[52] Case C–100/88 [1989] ECR 4285 at para 16.
[53] Case C–159/90 [1991] ECR I–4685.

so as to interfere with fundamental rights such as the rights encapsulated in Article 10 of the ECHR.[54] In *ERT*[55] the ECJ was of the same view.

I would suggest that it is not necessary in a democratic society to ban advertising of all books published by a person by virtue of their identity, or (worse) by virtue of the identity of another person with whom they are associated. A democratic society is characterised by "pluralism, tolerance and broadmindedness" as the European Court of Human Rights reminded us in *Handyside* v. *United Kingdom*.[56] Books are one of the most obvious ways in which ideas are transmitted in a democratic society. In a democratic society restrictions on their sale should be scrutinised with the greatest care.

Moreover, whatever the requirements of UK public policy may be, it is not necessary for there to be a ban on advertising through the media of satellite and cable *elsewhere* in the European Union.

In conclusion, I would suggest that there is scope for imaginative use of EC law, and therefore domestic law, to give effect to human rights, both freedom of movement as such and other rights such as freedom of expression. That process has only begun and its progress may falter, as it so far seems to have done in the case of Article 8a. However, in that process, I hope that it will be more widely appreciated that EC law is there not merely to protect commercial interests but also the human rights of all of us.

---

[54] See para 31: ". . . where national legislation falls within the field of application of Community law the Court . . . must provide the national court with all the elements of interpretation which are necessary in order to enable it to assess the compatibility of that legislation with the fundamental rights – as laid down in particular in the European Convention on Human Rights – the observance of which the Court ensures."

[55] Case C–260/89 [1991] ECR I–2929.

[56] Series A, No. 24 (1979–80) 1 EHRR 737, para. 49.

7

The Future of Public Interest Litigation[1]

Some people would say that the phrase "public interest litigation" contains a contradiction in terms. You may have seen that old cartoon which depicts two litigants who, in dispute over the ownership of a cow, are pulling on each end of it, while in the middle is a lawyer milking it. To many people, litigation is in no one's interest except lawyers'.

But there have always been lawyers who regard our profession as more than just a social club or a business, and who, in spite of ridicule (if not hatred or contempt), hope that they may contribute to the search for justice in some small, faltering way.

What do I mean by public interest litigation? If I were drafting a tax statute, I suppose, the interpretation section would say that it is litigation in the public interest – accurate but not particularly helpful. Alternatively, as a common lawyer, I might resort to judicial authority, at least in the form of a talk given by an American Supreme Court judge, Justice Marshall, in 1975:

"Public interest law seeks to fill some of the gaps in our legal system. Today's public interest lawyers have built upon the earlier successes [and I would add failures] of civil rights, civil liberties, and legal aid lawyers, but have moved into new areas. Before courts, administrative agencies and legislatures, they provide representation for a broad range of relatively powerless minorities – for example, to the mentally ill, to children, to the poor of all races. They also represent neglected interests that are widely shared by most of us as consumers, as workers, and as individuals in need of privacy and a healthy environment. These lawyers have, I believe, made an important contribution. They do not (nor should they) always prevail, but they have won many important victories for their clients. More fundamentally, perhaps, they have made our legal process work better. They have broadened the flow of information to decision-makers. They have made it possible for administrators, legislators, and judges to assess the impact of their decisions in terms of all affected interests. And, by opening doors to our legal system, they have moved us a little closer to the ideal of equal justice for all."[2]

---

[1] This essay is based on a seminar given at Queen Mary and Westfield College, London on 22 January 1997, which was chaired by Lord Lester of Herne Hill QC.

[2] Justice Marshall, "Financing Public Interest Law: The Role of the Organized Bar": Address to the Award of Merit Luncheon of the Bar Activities Section of the American Bar Association,

Public interest litigation is different from the normal dispute (however important) between two private parties about a sum of money: breach of a consumer contract, a car accident and so on. Public interest litigation often concerns either the public as a whole or large sections of it. It need not be the same as public law. For example, personal injury cases arising from disasters such as Hillsborough can often lead to large-scale litigation. Another kind of public interest case is where an important point of law arises which, while it may not affect a large number of people, it is in everyone's interest to resolve: for example, if the government has acted unlawfully in the way in which it has used the overseas aid budget.[3] A third type of public interest litigation is where a group seeks to act on behalf of interests that are not usually afforded legal personality or recognition at all: animals, the environment generally and future generations of people.

Public interest litigation has a special link to human rights. It provides part of the answer to the question I raised in Chapter 3. As I was suggesting then, the problem at the end of the twentieth century is not whether there are human rights but how to make them effective. This is particularly true of the newer generations of human rights, such as social and economic rights and environmental rights. These are often criticised as not being rights at all. It is said that they are non-justiciable because there is usually no individual who can claim to be the victim of some legal wrong. Very often, the way in which states try to implement this kind of human rights is through legislation which sets up agencies such as those that are supposed to administer the welfare state or to protect the environment. As I shall suggest later, the way in which courts may have a role in implementing such rights is if non-governmental organisations (NGOs) can use litigation to ensure that the state complies with its legal duties.

PUBLIC INTEREST LITIGATION IN THE PAST

Before I turn to the future of public interest litigation, I should consider its past. It is often thought that public interest litigation is the product of a relatively brief period in the history of the United States, from the 1950s to the 1970s.[4] As Harlow and Rawlings have reminded us:

10 August 1975, quoted in N Aron, *Liberty and Justice for All : Public Interest Law in the 1980s and Beyond* (Boulder, Westview Press, 1989) at 2. Before his appointment to the Bench, Thurgood Marshall was counsel to the NAACP – appearing most famously in *Brown* v. *Board of Education* 347 US 483 (1954) – and Solicitor-General in the administration of President Johnson.

[3] See, in the context of the misuse of the overseas aid budget, *R* v. *Secretary of State for Foreign Affairs, ex p. World Development Movement Ltd* [1995] 1 WLR 386 (DC).

[4] See, for example, R Dhavan, "Whose Law? Whose Interest?" in J Cooper & R Dhavan, *Public Interest Law* (Oxford, Basil Blackwell, 1986) at 12: "Phrases like 'public interest law' invite controversy. Pregnant with ambiguity they provoke both the reaction that such phrases can be made to mean anything as well as the response that we know what they mean but cannot really define them . . . 'Public interest law' is the product of a near-contemporary interlude in recent

"Nothing could be further from the truth. The use of law by pressure groups to achieve reform and to establish rights may be as old as pressure groups themselves. Long before the twentieth century, test cases and pressure-group litigation can be identified in Britain."[5]

Even in the USA, public interest litigation goes back at least to the turn of the century, a period known as the Progressive era. The best-known example of the Progressive lawyer was Louis Brandeis who (in between co-writing the most famous article on privacy[6] and becoming a Supreme Court judge) was busy defending the right of states to pass legislation for the protection of workers and giving his name to a kind of brief (about which more later). Public interest organisations have also helped to give life to the paper guarantees of the American Bill of Rights. For example, the First Amendment, which guarantees the right to freedom of speech, was enacted in 1791 but there was no Supreme Court authority on it until after the First World War. It is no accident that groups such as the American Civil Liberties Union have only been in existence since that date.[7]

Furthermore, public interest litigation has taken off in many jurisdictions now, including Canada[8] and Australia[9] and India. In the 1980s in particular, the Indian Supreme Court took it upon itself to reform procedural rules so as to make fundamental rights in the Constitution effective for the vast majority of Indian citizens. These included a willingness to receive informal letters of complaint as commencing legal proceedings and the appointment of commissions of inquiry in order to establish the facts in cases where systematic abuse of human rights was alleged. They also liberalised the rules on standing to allow direct challenges to be brought by NGOs. As a former Indian Attorney-General has put it:

"In India, there are numerous persons who, owing to poverty and severe social and economic handicaps, are totally unable to secure access to courts for enforcement of their rights which are violated with impunity. In view of these harsh realities, the Supreme Court, in order to ensure effective access to justice, has laid down that where judicial redress is sought for legal injury to the disadvantaged persons and downtrodden segments of society, any member of the public or an organisation

---

American history. Marketed as a compendium phrase to gather together a cluster of movements seeking to mobilize law and legal services on behalf of the disadvantaged, the phrase has come to acquire many meanings, not the least of which has been to encompass any espousal of the 'public interest' (often subjectively defined) by any persons or group. The export of the phrase beyond America has only added terminological confusion to its already varied use."

[5] C Harlow & R Rawlings, *Pressure Through Law* (London, Routledge, 1992) at 12.

[6] S D Warren & L D Brandeis, "The Right to Privacy" (1890) 4 Harv L Rev 193.

[7] See generally on the history of the American Civil Liberties Union: S Walker, *In Defense of American Liberties* (New York, OUP, 1990).

[8] See, for example, B McLachlin, "The Canadian Charter and the Democratic Process" in C Gearty & A Tomkins (eds), *Understanding Human Rights* (London, Mansell, 1996), ch. 2, especially at 32–3.

[9] For an outline of the work of the Public Interest Advocacy Centre, see its Annual Report for 1995: M Hogan, *Doing Public Justice* (Sydney, PIAC, 1996), especially at 5.

acting bona fide and not for oblique considerations can maintain an action on their behalf . . . Numerous under-trial prisoners languishing in jails for inordinately long periods have been released; persons treated like serfs and held in bondage have secured freedom and have been rehabilitated; inmates of care homes have been restored their humanity and the condition of stone workers in stone quarries and brick kilns has undergone a humanising change. Fundamental rights are no longer parchment promises but their enjoyment has become a living reality for some of these deprived and oppressed segments of Indian humanity."[10]

For those who want a detailed survey of the use of pressure through law in the United Kingdom, reference should be made to the book of that title by Harlow and Rawlings,[11] which traces the phenomenon of public interest litigation at least to the middle of the eighteenth century, to *Somerset v. Stewart* when Lord Mansfield CJ famously declared that "the black must be discharged" in deciding that a slave master could not seize his slave on English soil, since, as Lord Northington LC had put it, the air of England is "too pure for a slave to breathe". That decision was part of, and a spur to, the campaign for the abolition of slavery throughout the British Empire, which eventually bore fruit in 1833. *Somerset's* case is an early illustration of how litigation can be an effective element of a larger, campaigning strategy: that there need be no dichotomy between lobbying Parliament and going to court.[12]

Bringing test cases is not always productive at least in an immediate sense. For example, one of the first cases that were sponsored by the National Council for Civil Liberties (NCCL – now known as Liberty) in the mid-1930s, *Duncan v. Jones,*[13] was considered to be a disaster for civil liberties and might have been forgotten in the Quarter Sessions had it not been taken on appeal to the Divisional Court. There Lord Hewart CJ (and a former Conservative Attorney-General) was able to give an *ex tempore* judgment that extended the police's powers to ban peaceful assemblies. However, in the state of the authorities at the time, in particular *Beatty v. Gilbanks,*[14] it was understandable as a matter of law why *Duncan v. Jones* was taken up by NCCL. Moreover, as a matter of tactics, it was a way of highlighting the problem, to "awake realistic unease", as Sylvia Scaffardi, who with her partner Ronald

---

[10] S Sorabjee, "Obliging Government to Control Itself: Recent Developments in Indian Administrative Law" [1994] PL 39 at 49–50.

[11] C Harlow & R Rawlings, *supra* n. 5 at 12–17.

[12] Contrast C. Harlow, "Public Interest Litigation in England: The State of the Art" in J. Cooper and R. Dhavan, *supra* n. 4, ch. 4 at 133: "In a country where obedience to the law is (or has been) second nature, Trubek's point about legitimation needs to be kept in mind. Establishing in a court what the law is, and hence by inference always has been, may make a bad law harder, not easier, to dislodge. . . . [I]t must be remembered that, where resources are rationed, a victory for one client group of welfare services may have to be paid for by another and may produce a 'whiplash' effect from those who foot the bill. . . . In reality, law reform is a political activity which should be carried on in a political arena. . . . Politics and political action are not to be regarded as poor relations. Litigation is, and will always be, the junior partner."

[13] [1936] 1 KB 218 (DC).

[14] (1882) 9 QBD 308.

Kidd, helped to found NCCL in 1934, says in her autobiography.[15] Highlighting the injustice of the law can be a classic function of a test case strategy.[16]

Although it may not be a new phenomenon, public interest litigation has only recently been recognised for what it is in the United Kingdom. Our civil procedure is still based largely on the assumption that the function of the courts is to adjudicate on a particular person's rights. This private dispute model therefore has the following salient features:

(1) It is adversarial, usually bi-polar.
(2) The decision is reached only on the evidence before the court.
(3) Only the parties are entitled to put evidence before the court.
(4) Issues of law are usually decided on the basis of the submissions made for each party. There is some scope for independent research by the judge who has the time to do it but, even then, it usually provokes murmurs in the robing room that the judge has acted unfairly by going behind what counsel managed to unearth.
(5) Sometimes the assistance of an *amicus curiae* is sought. But only the Attorney-General or Official Solicitor appoint an *amicus*. Moreover, an *amicus* is usually sought only when one or both parties are unrepresented. Finally, while the *amicus* can make legal submissions, they are not entitled to place evidence before the court.[17]
(6) Costs usually follow the event, that is, the loser pays both sides' costs.
(7) The remedy given usually consists of an order binding only one person in favour of only one particular person.
(8) Only a party to the case may appeal.

This traditional model of civil procedure is not necessarily suited to coping with public interest litigation. Let me give three examples, one from each level of the judicial hierarchy. First, *Sutton LBC* v. *Davis*[18] which concerned the power of social services authorities to prevent registered childminders from smacking children. The local authority concerned decided not to appeal against the Divisional Court's decision against it. Accordingly, the law stood untested at a higher level, notwithstanding the disquiet felt by organisations

---

[15] S Scaffardi, *Fire under the Carpet: Working for Civil Liberties in the Thirties* (London, Lawrence and Wishart, 1986) at 100–1.
[16] That is not to say that one should set out to lose. Any advocate (and their clients) would prefer to win; sometimes, however, losing the legal battle can be an important part of a larger war.
[17] *R* v. *Leicester Justices, ex p. Barrow* [1991] 2 QB 260 at 289 (Lord Donaldson of Lymington MR).
[18] [1994] Fam 241.

concerned with children's rights. Secondly, perhaps a more famous case is *R v. Somerset County Council, ex p. Fewings*[19] which concerned the power of local authorities to ban stag-hunting on their land. While I have no doubt that the arguments were fully and eloquently put on each side, the issue was decided as a narrow one of statutory construction. Organisations concerned with animal welfare and animal rights did not participate in the court's proceedings. Thirdly and most famously, in *Gillick* v. *West Norfolk and Wisbech Area Health Authority*[20] the House of Lords adjudicated on the rights of children under sixteen to receive advice on contraception in a dispute between a government department and a moral campaigner. The Children's Legal Centre did ask for leave to intervene but this was refused without reasons being given.[21]

The problems are going to be exacerbated if and when the United Kingdom has a Bill of Rights enforceable in its own courts. This was the view of Henry LJ in *R* v. *Ministry of Defence, ex p. Smith*.[22] Parliament, with all its imperfections, at least has procedures that enable a variety of interests to have their say. People will rightly wonder whether courts can perform the role required of them under a Bill of Rights if their procedures are based on the private dispute model I outlined earlier.

THE ROLE OF NON-GOVERNMENTAL ORGANISATIONS

How should the courts react if public interest cases come before them in a systematic fashion? I would suggest that three principles should inform their approach: quality, pluralism and legitimacy. Quality, because their decisions should be as well-informed as possible. Pluralism because, in a liberal democracy, institutions that wield public power (as courts do) should allow all interests affected by them to participate in their processes. And that leads me to my third principle: legitimacy. Without legitimacy, the courts soon lose their moral authority and their claim to our respect and obedience. It is vital, there-

---

[19] (1995) 93 LGR 515 (CA).

[20] [1986] AC 112 (HL).

[21] Contrast the more pessimistic view of C Harlow, "Public Interest Litigation in England: The State of the Art" in Cooper & Dhavan *supra* n.4 at 118: "Those public interest lawyers who were relieved when the House of Lords, by a narrow majority, dismissed Mrs Gillick's action, should pause to reflect on the use of the courts to decide political questions of this type. No procedural tinkering by way of 'Brandeis briefs', appointment of the Attorney-General as amicus or permission to interest groups to present written amicus briefs can really solve the problem. The proper answer for wide-ranging issues of public concern lies in a Royal Commission, a Select Committee or a Committee of Inquiry like the Warnock Commission on Human Fertilization and Embryology. Administrative regulation based on informal consultation can also provide flexible, interim solutions which will usually lead in time to legislation."

[22] [1996] QB 517 at 564E–F: "If the Convention were to be made (or possibly be held to be) part of our domestic law, then in the exercise of the primary jurisdiction the court in, or for, it, a relatively novel constitutional position, might well ask for more material than the adversarial system normally provides, such as a 'Brandeis brief'."

fore, that they should be as well-informed and accountable to civil society as they can be consistent with their role as independent arbiters of fact and law, so that public confidence is retained.

Each of these principles would be better served if the role of groups (or NGOs) in litigation were openly recognised and valued. Although the issues that arise have general application to public law and even to private law, they have a particular relevance to human rights, especially (as I have suggested) the newer rights such as the right to a healthy environment. Often the way in which such rights will be effectively implemented is through *group litigation* and it is this concept that I would like to explore a little further. Groups can take part in litigation in three ways: first, by supporting individuals who wish to bring applications; secondly, by bringing applications in their own name; and thirdly, by intervening in cases already brought by others ("third party intervention").

Supporting Individuals

This is something which many groups are already familiar with. It is quite common to look for cases that have the factual merits on their side and will attract legal aid and match them to legal problems which it is in the public interest should be resolved, for example because they affect a large number of people or concern abuse of power by a public body.

The practical problem is that legal aid may not be available. There are two main reasons for this. First, the Legal Aid Board's Notes of Guidance[23] apply the "private client" and "cost-benefit" tests to the grant of legal aid. In some judicial review cases, the financial amount at stake for any one individual is relatively small, certainly not enough to justify a High Court case. This will be true of many social security cases. Secondly, the Notes of Guidance are averse to litigation that is brought in the public interest rather than to vindicate the private interests of an individual. They state that:

> "The purpose of legal aid is to support individuals who might otherwise be unable to take proceedings on account of their means . . . Legal aid is designed to assist those whom it finances in the course of litigation and not directly to assist other parties to the proceedings or other members of the public who are not parties to the proceedings in determining points of general interest . . . Indeed it would be an abuse of process to pursue proceedings with legal aid which are only of academic interest to lawyers and which no reasonable paying client would fund privately.

> There are cases where the existence of other claims can have a bearing on the merits or cost benefit of the application, particularly if the costs can be shared between claims in a multi-party action or test case, but public interest in the more general sense will rarely be a significant consideration in legal aid decisions."[24]

[23] See generally Legal Aid Board, *Legal Aid Handbook 1996/97* (London, Sweet & Maxwell, 1996) at 62–76.
[24] *Ibid.* at 68–9.

This is arguably a short-sighted approach. The Public Law Project has argued that, rather than have many individual cases funded haphazardly by the Legal Aid Board, there can be virtue in having a test case brought in the public interest, possibly by a group.[25]

One specific way in which an individual's application can be supported by a group that does not wish to bring a case in its own name is to place information before the court which will either help to resolve the issue of law or place it in context so that the importance of the case is brought out. Let me give some examples.

In social security cases, the Child Poverty Action Group (CPAG) sometimes describes the particular social security benefit in question, the number of people affected by the case and the way in which the benefit is operated, so that the court is aware of the context in which the legal issue arises.

In an immigration case,[26] the Refugee Legal Centre used an affidavit to inform the court of the limited resources that they and the United Nations High Commissioner for Refugees have to deal with a huge caseload. This was relevant to the question of whether fairness in practice required that the Home Office should be placed under a duty of disclosure in so-called "safe third country" cases.

Finally, in cases where there is a point of EC law raised, often the issue turns on whether the respondent's act, perhaps even a piece of legislation, is objectively justified and meets the test of proportionality when it *prima facie* infringes a fundamental right, such as the right to equality. Expert evidence as to social and economic issues is in such cases crucial to resolution of the legal issues. I shall come back to a vivid example of this, the *Seymour-Smith* case.

Information in support of an individual applicant can be placed before the court relatively cheaply in the form of an affidavit/affirmation, exhibiting if appropriate any published research or other documents that may assist the court. A recent example where this technique of assisting the court was deployed with practical effect is provided by *R* v. *Lord Chancellor, ex p. Witham,*[27] in which the Divisional Court held that Article 3 of the Supreme Court Fees (Amendment) Order 1996 was *ultra vires* because it had the effect of denying the constitutional right of access to the courts to people on low incomes without express authority from Parliament. The Court accepted affidavit evidence filed by the Public Law Project (a public interest organisation) which described categories of case where persons on very low incomes were prevented by Article 3 from taking action in the courts. Counsel for the Lord Chancellor had submitted that this evidence was irrelevant to the issue before the Court; but Laws J, with whose Judgment Rose LJ agreed, said:

[25] Public Law Project, *The Applicant's Guide to Judicial Review* (London, Sweet & Maxwell, 1995) at 80–3.

[26] *R* v. *Special Adjudicator, ex p. Abdi and Gawe* [1996] 1 WLR 298 (HL).

[27] [1997] 2 All ER 779.

"I see no reason not to accept what is said in these affidavits. In my view, it is clear on the evidence before us that there is a wide-ranging variety of situations in which persons on very low incomes are in practice denied access to the courts to prosecute claims or, in some circumstances, to take steps to resist the effects of claims brought against them."[28]

This case is a graphic illustration of how the full implications of an application which happens to be brought by one individual for the public interest can be brought to the attention of the court.

Applications by Groups In Their Own Name

A group may wish to bring a case in its own name because it wishes to attract publicity for its cause and simply supporting an individual applicant may not achieve this as well (Save Our Railways is a more catchy name for a case than Fred Bloggs). Sometimes, there may be no single applicant with standing and/or legal aid to bring the case. Finally, the case of a single applicant can become academic, for example because the particular case is settled, whereas a victory achieved by a group can bring practical benefits to a large class of people.

On the other hand, a group may be reluctant to bring an application in its own name because it may not have the resources to bring it, whereas an individual may get legal aid or it may not be able to afford the risk of paying the respondent's costs if it loses, whereas an individual on legal aid does not usually have to pay costs, at least in practice, since an applicant with no private funds is unlikely to be able to pay costs.

Before looking at the question of standing (or "*locus standi*") there is the logically prior issue of whether the group has legal capacity to bring an application at all. An unincorporated association does not have the capacity to bring applications for judicial review: see *R* v. *Darlington BC, ex p. Association of Darlington Taxi Owners*.[29] Other authorities suggest the contrary.[30] In practice, a properly advised group will either be incorporated (and so will have legal capacity) or will bring the application in its own name as well as in the name of individuals (such as its secretary or prominent members). In *Save Our Railways*, the first applicant was the unincorporated group but there were many individual applicants as well: the capacity issue does not seem to have been a problem.

The courts are increasingly willing to permit groups to bring applications for judicial review in their own name. They must, like individuals, satisfy the test of "sufficient interest" in section 31(3) of the Supreme Court Act 1981 and RSC Ord. 53, r. 3(7).

---

[28] At 782 a–b
[29] [1994] COD 424 (Auld J).
[30] K Gledhill, "Standing, Capacity and Unincorporated Assocations" [1996] JR 67.

In the last fifteen years, there has been a transformation in the law of stand-ing, although the path has not always been a smooth one. The process began with Lord Diplock's eloquent statement in *R* v. *Inland Revenue Commis-sioners, ex p. National Federation of Self Employed*:

> "It would, in my view, be a grave lacuna in our system of public law if a pressure group, like the federation, or even a single public-spirited taxpayer, were prevented by outdated technical rules of locus standi from bringing the matter to the attention of the court to vindicate the rule of law and get the unlawful conduct stopped."[31]
> [1982] AC 617 at 644E

The trend at least since the *Rose Theatre* case has been to take a more "lib-eral" view (the word used by Rose LJ in *World Development Movement*). The law reports include cases brought by CPAG; Greenpeace; Friends of the Earth; World Development Movement; Save Our Railways; and JCWI.[32] The factors which the court will take into account are the importance of maintaining the rule of law; the importance of the issue raised by the application; the likely absence of any other "responsible" challenger; the nature of the breach of duty against which relief is sought; and the expertise and experience of the appli-cant body.[33]

The new approach to standing places more emphasis on permitting serious groups to raise important questions so that the High Court may exercise its supervisory jurisdiction to see that power is not being exceeded or abused, rather than to see whether individual legal rights or interests are affected. It is possible therefore for a group to bring what is in substance a "public inter-est" application for judicial review. Peter Cane has called this a "sea-change in judicial attitudes".[34]

This approach is also reflected in the report in 1996 by a working party established by JUSTICE and the Public Law Project chaired by Laws J, *A Matter of Public Interest* where it is said:

> "In our view, this supports the true nature of the court's role in public law cases

---

[31] [1982] AC 617 at 644E.

[32] Recent cases have unequivocally embraced the notion of "public interest standing": see *R* v. *Secretary of State for Foreign and Commonwealth Affairs, ex p. World Development Movement Ltd* [1995] 1 WLR 386 at 392G–396C and 403E; *R* v. *HM Inspectorate of Pollution ex p. Greenpeace (No. 2)* [1994] 4 All ER 329 at 346G–352A; *R* v. *Secretary of State for Employment ex p. Equal Opportunities Commission* [1995] AC 1; and *R* v. *Secretary of State for Social Services ex p. CPAG* [1990] 2 QB 540 at 556G *per* Woolf LJ.

[33] See especially *R* v. *Secretary of State for Foreign Affairs, ex p. World Development Movement Ltd*, where these factors and the leading authorities are listed.

[34] See further P Cane, "Standing Up for the Public" [1995] Public Law 276 especially at 287: "This view of the proper function of judicial review is diametrically opposed to the traditional emphasis of the courts on individuals. But the willingness of the courts to allow public interest challenges to public decisions suggests just such a sea-change in judicial attitudes and might jus-tify a prediction that public interest and associational applications for judicial review will grow in numbers and importance in the years to come."

which is not to determine the rights of individual applicants but to ensure that public bodies do not exceed or abuse their powers."[35]

Both the Law Commission and the JUSTICE/PLP report recommend that the rules should expressly permit groups to bring applications for judicial review in their own name where it is in the public interest. This reform would confirm the present law rather than extend it.

However, there is a practical problem for groups which bring applications in their own names: costs normally follow the event in judicial review cases. It is true that sometimes the courts have been prepared to order that there should be no order as to costs even though an application for judicial review has failed.

In a number of cases going back at least to *Liversidge* v. *Anderson*[36] the Court has acceded to an argument that costs should not be ordered against an unsuccessful party because of the significant public interest in the resolution of the questions raised by the particular proceedings. Recent examples are *Greenpeace* and *JCWI* at first instance.

However, the trend has not been in one direction only. In a number of recent cases the Court has refused to depart from the ordinary rule that costs follow the event, in spite of submissions to the contrary: see, for example, *R* v. *Ministry of Defence ex p. Smith*[37] (the gays in the military case); *R* v. *Secretary of State for the Environment ex p. Friends of the Earth*[38] (concerning the quality of drinking water in the UK, and the government's obligations pursuant to the Drinking Water Directive); and especially *R* v. *Intervention Board for Agricultural Produce ex p. Fish Producers' Organisation Limited*[39] where the Court of Appeal held that the normal costs rule was applicable to the costs of a reference to the European Court of Justice which had had to be made in the course of judicial review proceedings. Ralph Gibson LJ said[40] that "it is in my experience common that the court's discretion is not applied differently or in any special way in circumstances where the costs arise in judicial review."

Even if an application for judicial review succeeds, or there is no order as to costs at the end of the substantive hearing, the reality is that groups are likely to be deterred from bringing applications unless they know *at an early stage* that they will not be liable for costs whichever side wins. This is why

---

[35] At page 3. I should declare an interest: I was a member of this working party. As the Law Commission puts it in its 1994 Report, *Administrative Law: Judicial Review and Statutory Appeals* (Law Com No. 226) at para. 2.5: "The public interest in the vindication of the rule of law underpins the very existence of the prerogative jurisdiction and its supervisory role over inferior courts and decision-makers." This distinctive, constitutional function of the High Court's supervisory jurisdiction gives rise to an essential difference between judicial review and ordinary private litigation, noted by the Law Commission at para. 2.1 of its Report: "Judicial review often involves values and policy interests, which must be balanced against and may transcend the individual interests which are normally the subject of litigation between private citizens."

[36] [1942] AC 206.

[37] [1996] QB 517.

[38] (unreported, 25 May 1995, CA).

[39] [1993] 1 CMLR 707.

[40] *Ibid.* at para. 13.

the suggestion has been made that the court should make a "protective costs order" if it grants leave to move for judicial review in a case which is brought to its attention in the public interest.

A Joint Opinion by Leading and Junior Counsel was obtained in 1996 by CPAG on this question.[41] Despite the conflicting authorities on the question of the costs of litigation brought in the public interest, the Opinion states both that there is *already* a power in the court to make a protective costs order and that, in an appropriate case, the Court should exercise its discretion to make a protective costs order where:

(1) The substantive point is (objectively) one of general *public* importance which ought to be litigated, for example because it concerns the legality of governmental action and/or because it affects a large number of people.

(2) The point of law would not otherwise be litigated, for example because none of those affected has the resources to fund proceedings personally or is able to secure legal aid.

(3) The applicant is the best representative of the interests directly affected by the challenged decision or measure and/or is well-placed, because of its expertise in the area, to bring the issue before the Court.

(4) The respondent is able to, and should, bear its own costs whatever the outcome of the case, since it is a public body and it is in the public's interest that the issue of law raised should be resolved.

These factors are similar to those which influenced the Ontario Law Reform Commission in 1989 to propose that:

". . . the applicant could ask for a decision on costs *at any point* in a public interest case and the court would be prevented from ordering costs against the applicant if the following conditions were met:

*the case involves issues whose importance extends beyond the immediate interests of the parties involved

*the applicant has no personal, proprietary or pecuniary interest in the outcome of the case

*the respondent has a clearly superior capacity to bear the costs of the proceedings."[42]

It can be argued that to recognise that a group has standing to bring a particular application for judicial review because it is in the public interest that it should be brought without making a protective costs order is to take away with one hand what has been given with the other. This is why, in spite of the liberalisation of standing rules, the law reports are not replete with applications that are brought directly by NGOs.

---

[41] Again I should declare an interest: the Opinion was written by Alan Moses QC (as he then was), Murray Hunt, Andrew Tabachnik and me.

[42] See the JUSTICE/PLP Report *supra* n. 35 at 14 (*emphasis added*).

Unfortunately, recent reports that have considered reform of public law procedures have not expressly supported the concept of protective costs orders. The Law Commission recommended that there should be a power to award costs out of central funds in public interest cases.[43] Lord Woolf's report on "Access to Justice" makes a similar recommendation, failing which it suggests that the court should have a discretion not to award costs against an unsuccessful group applicant, at least where there would be substantial hardship.[44] This has been the subject of some criticism for not favouring protective costs orders, not least because the recommendation probably goes no further than current law and practice anyway.[45]

With great respect to Lord Woolf, I would suggest that the time is ripe for express recognition of the importance of protective costs orders.

THIRD PARTY INTERVENTION

A group may want to intervene in an application begun by another person because it may have been begun without the support or even knowledge of an interested group which may want to offer its support to the applicant and/or assist the court; it may raise issues affecting the group's purposes which require *opposition* by the group; or the group may have particular expertise that should be placed before the court because otherwise the full significance of the issues will not be appreciated, for example, if there is a human rights dimension to the case.

Indeed, as Lord Lester has written, the Georgetown Conclusions on the effective protection of human rights through law recommend that courts should allow themselves to be assisted by well focused submissions from NGOs such as Interights, especially in novel cases where international and comparative law and practice may be relevant.[46]

At present, there is only limited scope for formal intervention as a third party in public law proceedings:

(1) Persons "directly affected" must be served with the papers if leave is granted.[47] Those served become parties to the case. Groups are rarely

---

[43] Law Com No. 226, *Administrative Law: Judicial Review and Statutory Appeals*, para 10.6.

[44] Lord Woolf MR, "Report on Access to Justice" (1996) at 255, para 22: "I agree with the Law Commission that legislation should confer a discretion on the court to order costs to be paid out of central funds where it is in the public interest that proceedings should be brought. If this recommendation is not implemented I recommend that the court should have a discretion not to order an unsuccessful party to pay the other party's costs, on the grounds that the proceedings have been brought in the public interest. Initially the discretion should only be exercised where there would otherwise be substantial hardship."

[45] See e.g. S Cragg, "Lord Woolf and JR" [1996] JR 236 at 238, para 14: "At present, at least, public interest groups would contest Lord Woolf's view that judicial review applications 'should involve relatively modest expenditure by the parties'."

[46] Lord Lester of Herne Hill QC, "The Georgetown Conclusions on the effective protection of human rights through law" [1996] PL 562 at 565, para 12.

going to be directly affected, especially since that phrase has been given a restricted meaning by the House of Lords.[48]

(2) Persons may be permitted by the court to be heard *in opposition* to an application for judicial review.[49] Again, this is unlikely to be of interest to many groups, but has been important when, for example, a challenge is brought against attempts to stop exports of live animals: in *R v. Coventry City Council, ex p. Phoenix Aviation*[50] Compassion in World Farming were represented at the oral hearing.

(3) In the Court of Appeal it is provided by the rules that persons who are not parties to the appeal may be served at the court's discretion.[51]

(4) In the House of Lords rules there is the most explicit recognition of the concept of third-party intervention.[52] In practice the House has been reluctant to give leave but this may change after *R v. Khan (Sultan)*[53] (a criminal case) in which Liberty made a written submission to the House on the impact of the European Convention on Human Rights on that case and were thanked in terms by Lord Nolan for assisting the House.

The rules of the European Court of Justice and the European Court of Human Rights do permit third-party intervention. British organisations such as Liberty have taken full advantage of this especially in Strasbourg.

The JUSTICE/PLP report "A Matter of Public Interest" recommends that the Rules of the Supreme Court should be changed to permit third-party intervention in the public interest where it would assist the court. Control over such intervention would be exercised by the court. Leave would be needed. Submissions would normally only be permitted in writing, with a maximum of twenty pages set. The court could impose such terms and conditions as it thinks fit, including a term that additional costs incurred as a result of the intervention should be paid by the intervenor. The phrase "third-party intervention" is used instead of the more familiar *amicus curiae* which is used in countries such as the USA and Australia because that phrase has a distinctive meaning in our system (it refers to counsel appointed by the Attorney-General or the Official Solicitor, usually at the request of the Court).

Whatever the label used, this reform would herald the way to a new and important role for groups which will have a responsibility to act as friends of the court, like their counterparts in other countries. It should also make it more likely that social and economic information finds its way to the court's attention: in the USA this is called a "Brandeis brief".

---

[47] RSC Ord. 53, r. 5(3).

[48] *R v. Rent Officer, ex p. Muldoon* [1996] 3 All ER 498 (HL).

[49] RSC Ord. 53, r. 9(1).

[50] [1995] 3 All ER 37 (DC).

[51] RSC Ord. 59, r. 8(1).

[52] Practice Directions and Standing Orders Applicable to Civil Appeals, House of Lords (January 1996) Direction 34.1.

[53] [1996] 3 WLR 162 (HL).

In the USA perhaps the most famous use of the Brandeis brief was in *Brown* v. *Board of Education*[54] in which the Supreme Court held that racial segregation of schools was unconstitutional. The case was brought with the support of the NAACP, one of the best known NGOs in the USA: the Court mentions in footnote 11 to its Opinion the sociological information that was placed before it which showed that segregation had a damaging psychological impact on black children, so that the notorious doctrine of "separate but equal" had to be overturned.[55]

This may seem a long way from English law. However, let me give an example from our own law reports: *R* v. *Secretary of State for Employment, ex p. Seymour-Smith*.[56] In that case, the issue was whether the rule that employees have to have been employed for at least two years before they enjoy protection from unfair dismissal constituted indirect sex discrimination. There was before the court information as to the objective justification for the rules: although the Divisional Court and the Court of Appeal differed in the outcome of the proceedings which turned on another point, to do with the meaning of indirect discrimination, neither court was impressed with the government's data. Applying the approach of the House of Lords in the *EOC* case they held that the alleged impact on the job market did not objectively justify the indirect discrimination.[57] If our courts can deal with this kind of sensitive case, as they must, when a Community law right is invoked, why should they not be competent to deal with cases under a Bill of Rights in the future?

CONCLUSIONS

In conclusion, the future of public interest litigation will, I hope be a bright one. NGOs will not only have standing to bring applications in their own name: they will, in proper cases, be protected by a costs order at an early stage of proceedings. NGOs will also regularly act as "friends of the court" by mak-

---

[54] 347 US 483 (1954).

[55] See W L Taylor, "Litigation as a Tool of Empowerment for the Poor", Address to the National Neighbourhood Coalition Conference, 25 November 1985, quoted in N Aron, *Liberty and Justice for All: Public Interest Law in the 1980s and Beyond* (Boulder, Westview Press, 1989) at 97: "[*Brown* v. *Board of Education*] rekindled the hopes of black people and gave new energy to the programs of established organizations, notably the NAACP . . . the implicit message of the *Brown* decision was that by their own efforts even the people most discriminated against in this [American] society could make the system work for them. If it is sadly true that the message still rings hollow in 1985 for millions of black people who are worse off in this country, for many, many others, *Brown* was the event that ultimately enabled them to gain control over their own lives."

[56] [1995] ICR 889 at 907 (DC) and 954 (CA).

[57] The actual decision of the Court of Appeal – to make a declaration in favour of the applicants – was reversed by the House of Lords: [1997] 2 All ER 273. However, the House reached its conclusion on this aspect of the case on agreed preliminary issues of law and was not invited to, and did not, comment on whether the approach of the courts below was correct. The House made a reference to the European Court of Justice raising certain questions about the interpretation and application of Article 119 of the EC Treaty.

ing submissions in cases that affect many, diverse interests and in particular in human rights cases. Indeed there may in the future be a Human Rights Commission one of whose functions could be to assist a court in cases where a decision might place the United Kingdom in breach of its international obligations on human rights.[58] Finally, it may even be that NGOs will in suitable cases be permitted to take cases to the appellate courts where a point of law of general importance is raised but, for reasons of cost or otherwise, the actual parties to the case do not wish to take the case further. This is not necessarily as heretical as it may sound. In the criminal context, the Attorney-General has for many years had the power to refer a case to the Court of Appeal (Criminal Division) where the particular defendant has been acquitted but a point of law affecting others arises. There is no question of the particular case being re-opened but the point of law can be determined to assist in other cases.

Whatever the exact nature of the reforms that occur over the next few years, I doubt if our civil procedure will remain the same in the twenty-first century. It will have to be modified if it is properly to meet the needs of public interest litigation. And, as it does so, it will, to adapt the words of Justice Marshall, "by opening doors to our legal system . . . [move] us a little closer to the ideal of equal justice for all".[59] If I might end on a personal note, there is a poem by the Indian Nobel Laureate, Rabindranath Tagore, in which he speaks of:

". . . Justice weeping silently and furtively at power misused,
    No hope of redress."[60]

I hope that we can all play a part in seeing that Justice need no longer weep.

---

[58] This is suggested in a Consultation Paper issued by the Institute for Public Policy Research in December 1996: see further S Spencer & I Bynoe, "A Human Rights Commission for the UK: The Options" [1997] EHRLR 152. It is also suggested by the Report of the Joint Consultative Committee on Constitutional Reform established by the Labour and Liberal Democrat parties (March 1997). See further *supra* Chapter 2.

[59] Justice Marshall, "Financing Public Interest Law: The Role of the Organized Bar": Address to the Award of Merit Luncheon of the Bar Activities Section of the American Bar Association, 10 August 1975, quoted in N Aron, *Liberty and Justice for All : Public Interest Law in the 1980s and Beyond* (Boulder, Westview Press, 1989) at 2.

[60] R Tagore, *Selected Poems* (Harmondsworth, Penguin, 1987) at 96.

Select Bibliography

Aron, N, *Liberty and Justice for All : Public Interest Law in the 1980s and Beyond* (Boulder, Westview Press, 1989).

Beloff, M J & Mountfield, H, "Unconventional Behaviour? Judicial Uses of the European Convention in English Law" [1996] EHRLR 467.

Lord Bingham of Cornhill CJ, "The European Convention on Human Rights: Time to Incorporate" in R Gordon & R Wilmot-Smith (eds), *Human Rights in the United Kingdom* (Oxford, Clarendon Press, 1996) ch. 1.

Lord Bingham of Cornhill CJ, "Should There Be a Law to Protect Rights of Personal Privacy?" [1996] EHRLR 450.

Bobbio, N, *The Age of Rights* (tr. Cameron, Oxford, Polity Press, 1996).

Lord Browne-Wilkinson, "The Infiltration of a Bill of Rights" [1992] PL 397.

Cane, P, "Standing Up for the Public" [1995] Public Law 276.

Clark, J C D, *The Language of Liberty 1660–1832* (Cambridge, Cambridge University Press, 1994).

Cooper, J & Dhavan, R, *Public Interest Law* (Oxford, Basil Blackwell, 1986).

de Búrca, G, "Fundamental Human Rights and the Reach of EC Law" (1993) 13 OJLS 283.

Dworkin, R, *Taking Rights Seriously* (London, Duckworth, 1977).

Dworkin, R, *A Bill of Rights for Britain* (London, Chatto & Windus, 1990).

Eady, D, "A Statutory Right to Privacy" [1996] EHRLR 243.

Ely, J H, *Democracy and Distrust* (Cambridge, Massachusetts, Harvard University Press, 1980).

Grief, N, "The Domestic Impact of the European Convention on Human Rights as Mediated through Community Law" [1991] PL 555.

Harlow, C & Rawlings, R, *Pressure Through Law* (London, Routledge, 1992).

Hunt, M, *Using Human Rights Law in English Courts* (Oxford, Hart Publishing, 1997).

Lord Irvine of Lairg, "Judges and Decision-Makers: The Theory and Practice of *Wednesbury* Review" [1996] PL 59.

Lord Irvine of Lairg, "The Legal System and Law Reform Under Labour" in D Bean (ed), *Law Reform for All* (London, Blackstone, 1996) ch. 1.

Keane, J, *Tom Paine: A Political Biography* (London, Bloomsbury, 1995).

Kentridge, S, "Parliamentary Supremacy and the Judiciary under a Bill of Rights: Some Lessons from the Commonwealth" [1997] PL 96.

Klug, F, "Human Rights as Secular Ethics" in R Gordon & R Wilmot-Smith (eds), *Human Rights in the United Kingdom* (Oxford, Clarendon Press, 1996), ch. 5.

Sir John Laws, "Is the High Court the Guardian of Fundamental Constitutional Rights?" [1993] PL 59.

Sir John Laws, "The Constitution: Morals and Rights" [1996] PL 622.

Lester, A, "Fundamental Rights: the United Kingdom Isolated?" [1984] PL 46.

Lester, A, "English Judges as Law Makers" [1993] PL 269.

Lord Lester of Herne Hill, "The Georgetown Conclusions on the effective protection of human rights through law" [1996] PL 562.

Lord Lester of Herne Hill, "First Steps Towards a Constitutional Bill of Rights" [1997] EHRLR 124.

Lukes, S, "Five Fables About Human Rights" in S Shute & S. Hurley (eds), *On Human Rights: The Oxford Amnesty Lectures* (New York, Basic Books, 1993).

Lukes, S, *The Curious Enlightenment of Professor Caritat* (London, Verso, 1996).

McLachlin, B, "The Canadian Charter and the Democratic Process" in C Gearty & A Tomkins (eds), *Understanding Human Rights* (London, Mansell, 1996) ch. 2.

Marston, G, "The United Kingdom's Part in the Preparation of the European Convention on Human Rights, 1950" (1993) 42 ICLQ 796.

Milton, J, "*Areopagitica*" *in Complete English Poems, Of Education, Areopagitica* 4th edn (London, J. M. Dent & Sons, 1990).

Paine, T, *The Rights of Man* (original 1791–2) (Harmondsworth, Penguin, 1984).

Ryssdall, R, "The Coming of Age of the European Convention on Human Rights" [1996] EHRLR 18.

Scaffardi, S, *Fire under the Carpet: Working for Civil Liberties in the Thirties* (London, Lawrence and Wishart, 1986).

Sir Stephen Sedley "Human Rights: A Twenty First Century Agenda", [1995] PL 386.

Sorabjee, S, "Obliging Government to Control Itself: Recent Developments in Indian Administrative Law" [1994] PL 39.

Wadham, J, "Bringing Rights Half-way Home" [1997] EHRLR 141.

Walker, S, *In Defense of American Liberties* (New York, OUP, 1990).

Zander, M, *A Bill of Rights?* 4th edn (London, Sweet & Maxwell, 1997).

Index